The TAROT TRUMPS

The TAROT TRUMPS

Cosmos in Miniature

The Structure and Symbolism of the Twenty-Two Tarot Trump Cards

by

JOHN SHEPHARD

THE AQUARIAN PRESS
Wellingborough, Northamptonshire

First published 1985

British Library Cataloguing in Publication Data

Shephard, John
    The tarot trumps: cosmos in miniature.
    1. Tarot
    I. Title
    133.3'2424   BF1879.T2

ISBN 0-85030-450-4

*The Aquarian Press is part of the
Thorsons Publishing Group*

Printed and bound in Great Britain

Contents

Illustrations

Introduction

The tarot has fascinated many writers. It was Court de Gébelin, a French antiquary, who first proclaimed the mystery of the cards when he announced in 1781 that they were the remains of an Ancient Egyptian book of wisdom. The mists surrounding their origin have cleared a little since his day and we can see now that the earliest tarot cards came from the Italy of the Renaissance, the source of so much in European art and culture. Nevertheless there is still something of an air of mystery about them. They are strange to us because they present a world picture in many ways foreign to the beliefs about the nature of things which we have come to accept today.

Tarot was a game of cards which took the hierarchy of the universe for its theme. The sequence of trumps of increasing value reflected the grades of the cosmic hierarchy, the steps up the ladder of being. It was both a game and a highly systematic allegory of the proper order of things as the fifteenth century saw it, a cosmos in miniature. This book will try to show the structure of that cosmic hierarchy.

If we look at a pack of ordinary playing cards, a standard 52-card bridge pack, they offer a simple picture of society. First there are the pip cards, ten grades of commoner in four suits, four nations if you wish. Above these are the Knaves, the bold bad barons. Finally there are the Kings and Queens at the head of each

suit, each court. The pack presents a child's-eye view of the social structure, as it were.

The tarot trumps build on and extend this simple structure. Above the Kings and Queens of the court cards are placed *The Popess* and *The Empress, The Emperor* and *The Pope,* supra-national figures but still purely human, inhabiting the world of everyday life, the world of human personality.

Above them comes the world of the soul, with figures like *Justice, Fortune,* and *Death.* Here the figures have become allegorical rather than human.

Finally there is the world of the life beyond death, with *The Devil* lying in wait to pounce on the intemperate soul, while the more prudent and circumspect could hope that after the Last *Judgement* they would bask in eternal glory in a new *World,* the New Jerusalem, the City of God.

It is because they have this quality of universality — the whole of Heaven and Hell and Earth is represented in them — that tarot cards have come in our day to serve also for divination. The little images have a curious power. They provide a framework within which imagination and fantasy, the picture-making of the human mind, can play freely.

To understand this framework we shall have to look at the world picture of fifteenth-century Italy, the conventional beliefs about the nature of the universe held by the average more or less educated man or woman who would have absorbed something from a formal schooling but probably rather more from the whole background of daily life and pageantry.

For a society that was professedly Christian, this world picture turns out to be a rather surprising one. At the apex of the cosmic hierarchy the supreme throne was of course occupied by God the Father. With him were proper bands of attendant angels, but these were much occupied in praising him, and the day-to-day administration of the universe was regarded as being carried out by more mundanely-minded figures, in shapes and forms found in medieval allegorical poetry but really survivors from the world of classical antiquity. We meet beings like Astraea, Goddess of Justice, and Fortuna with her Wheel; and there is Natura, planning the continuation of the species which will be brought about by Cupid. But it was the seven planetary gods, the departmental Governors appointed by God the Father, who were the real powers behind the scenes.

In the highly sophisticated society of the Italy of the Renaissance, it is not to be thought that these figures were taken as having actual physical existence. They were consciously accepted as allegorical personifications. They were regarded as symbolizing the basic forces and energies and appetites at work in the universe, and their myths were taken as allegories of the parts these forces played in the world of human nature.

We have always to remember the great revival of interest in classical antiquity which was so strong a mark of the Renaissance. The myths and legends of Greece and Rome, known through the ancient poets and Ovid and Virgil in particular, once again became favourite subjects in art. In at least one place a classical myth will provide an essential key to the understanding of the tarot.

The tarot trumps show us a world picture drawn from Christian teaching and from pagan mythology, from medieval astrology

and from allegorical poetry, all mixed together in an age that itself mingled belief in these things with unbelief. It is the very strangeness of this mixture, this cosmos in miniature, that gives the tarot its special fascination.

The tarot packs
There are many kinds of tarot pack. In this book we shall be concerned with the traditional 21-trump kinds used in Southern Europe. As we are trying to discover their original structure, we shall look chiefly at those which were in existence at early dates; later packs will be discussed only incidentally.

Illustrations of many early cards and a great deal of valuable background information can be found in *The Encyclopedia of Tarot*, vol. 1, by Stuart R. Kaplan (New York, 1978). References to this will be abbreviated to 'Kaplan'.

Differences of subject in early 21-trump packs, that is to say, differences in what is depicted on the individual trump cards, are not in general very numerous, and even when they do occur there is usually not much difficulty in seeing how the trumps of different packs correspond to each other. For our purposes here differences solely of regional style or artistic manner will not usually be important, nor will differences in the court or pip cards.

Differences in the order of the trumps are much more important, and provide a much more useful basis for classification of packs than the differences of subject. However, in the earliest packs the trumps did not bear numbers as an integral part of their designs, so there may be some doubt about their proper order.

The problem of the order of the trumps has been very fully examined by Michael Dummett in his important book, *The Game of Tarot* (London, 1980), which will be referred to here as 'Dummett'. According to the kinds of order of the trumps he distinguishes three main types or groups, within each of which there may still be minor differences of order between particular packs.

His first type, A, includes an order indicated in a fifteenth-century pack usually called the Charles VI cards and which, with some variations, is also followed in several other early packs, as well as in the present-day Tarocco of Bologna. I shall call this type the 'Charles VI' order. It seems the most likely to have been the original order.

His second type, B, covers what was probably a slightly later kind of order. This is found in a list appearing in a fifteenth-century volume of sermons discovered by Robert Steele, extracts from which he published in 1900. I call this, and minor variants, the 'Steele' order. It does not seem ever to have been very widely used, and it is not represented by any present-day type of pack.

His third type, C, represents the kind of order found in by far the largest number of later types of pack, including the so-called Marseille pattern. This order is found in a French pack of 1557, but it was almost certainly in use in Italy earlier than that.

Since this third type eventually became very widely accepted I shall call it here the 'Standard' order. It is with this type of order that we shall be mainly concerned in this book, and it is this type which is to be understood as being meant when not otherwise indicated.

In addition to their twenty-one trumps, all these three types normally also had *The Fool*, which was usually an unnumbered card. To save constant repetition, references to 21-trump packs should be taken to imply the presence of a *Fool* as well.

There is one further kind of pack that will sometimes be mentioned here, the Minchiate, which had forty trumps plus *The Fool*. Twenty of these trumps may be said to correspond, broadly, to those of 21-trump packs, omitting *The Popess;* but twenty further trumps have been added: four more Virtues, the four Elements, and the twelve signs of the Zodiac.

The Minchiate pack was in use mainly in the area around Florence. Exactly when it was invented is not known, but it was certainly in existence by the mid-sixteenth century. While it is no longer in general use today, the main importance of the Minchiate so far as this book is concerned lies in the fact that the designs remained exceptionally stable over the years, the earliest known Minchiate cards being closely similar to those in use some hundreds of years later. As it appears to have come into being as a result of twenty new trumps having been added, in a consecutive block, to twenty trumps of existing type it seems likely that the Minchiate cards in effect preserve features of design and order which were already in use at that time in early 21-trump packs.

The Charles VI Order

The Fool

*		The Magician (Bagatto)
*	1	The Popess
*	2	The Empress
	3	The Emperor
	4	The Pope
	5	Love (The Lovers or The Lover)
	6	Temperance
	7	Fortitude
	8	Justice
	9	The Chariot
*	10	The Wheel of Fortune
	11	The Hermit (The Old Man or The Hunchback)
	12	The Hanged Man (The Traitor)
	13	Death
*	14	The Devil
	15	The Tower
*	16	The Star
	17	The Moon
	18	The Sun
	19	The World
	20	Judgement (The Angel)

The fifteenth-century cards known as the Charles VI pack are in the Bibliothèque Nationale in Paris. Some of them are illustrated in Figures 1 and 2. Monochrome illustrations of all can be found in Kaplan, p.112-116. The cards marked with an asterisk are not actually present in that pack, but that they originally existed may be presumed from comparison with other sets broadly of this type, particularly an early uncut sheet in the National Gallery of Art, Washington, D.C. (Kaplan, p.130-131. Dummett, plate 6).

The cards themselves do not bear any written names. Those given here are English versions of the Italian or French names commonly in use, with some alternative names in brackets. Their numbering is discussed in Chapter 3.

The distinguishing characteristic of this type of order is that the three Virtues, *Temperance, Fortitude, Justice,* are always found together as a group, though in some packs the relative order of the three and their exact position may differ a little from the list given above. Sometimes the numbering may start with *The Magician* as No. 1. Some of the cards may be left unnumbered.

The present-day Tarocco Bolognese and Tarocco Siciliano are derived from this type.

The Steele Order

1 The Bagatelle (= The Magician, or Bagatto)
2 The Empress
3 The Emperor
4 The Popess
5 The Pope
6 Temperance
7 Love
8 The Triumphal Chariot, or the Little World
9 Fortitude
10 The Wheel
11 The Hunchback (= The Hermit)
12 The Hanged Man
13 Death
14 The Devil
15 The Lightning (= The Tower)
16 The Star
17 The Moon
18 The Sun
19 The Angel (= Judgement)
20 Justice
21 The World, that is, God the Father

0 The Fool

This order is found in a list in a sermon written by an Italian friar probably in the late fifteenth century, and published by Robert Steele in *Archaeologia,* vol. 57 (London, 1900). The manuscript list is reproduced in Kaplan, facing p.1. The names of the cards listed above are translations of those actually given in the sermon. Those in brackets have been added to indicate equivalents in standard packs.

The distinguishing characteristic of this type of order is that the three Virtues are not consecutive, as they were in the Charles VI order, but are split up, with *Temperance* still No. 6 but *Fortitude* now No. 9 and *Justice* No. 20. *The World* is now No. 21.

Imperfect sheets from the late fifteenth or early sixteenth century, in the Metropolitan Museum of Art, New York, broadly follow this type of order (Dummett, plate 5, and Kaplan, p.125).

The Standard Order
(The Marseille Tarot, etc.)

The Fool

1 The Magician
2 The Popess
3 The Empress
4 The Emperor
5 The Pope
6 Love (The Lovers or The Lover)
7 The Chariot
8 Justice
9 The Hermit (The Old Man)
10 The Wheel of Fortune
11 Fortitude
12 The Hanged Man (The Traitor)
13 Death
14 Temperance
15 The Devil
16 The Tower
17 The Star
18 The Moon
19 The Sun
20 Judgement (The Angel)
21 The World

This is the order found in by far the largest number of packs. As in the Steele order, the Virtues are split up, but here *Justice* is No. 8, *Fortitude* No. 11 and *Temperance* No. 14.

There are a number of variant packs which show differences of subject in some of the cards. Thus *The Pope* may be replaced by a *Jupiter,* and *The Popess* by a *Juno.* There are also occasional minor differences of order.

In modern packs designed mainly for divination *Justice* and *Fortitude* are often transposed. This change is a purely modern innovation, made for occultist reasons, and is not found in any of the older packs.

The Minchiate Order

The Fool

1 Papa uno   (= The Magician)
2 Papa due   (= The Empress?)
3 Papa tre   (= The Emperor?)   *Papi*
4 Papa quattro   (= The Pope?)
5 Papa cinque   (= Love)
6 Temperance
7 Fortitude
8 Justice
9 The Wheel of Fortune
10 The Chariot
11 The Hunchback (The Hermit)
12 The Hanged Man (The Traitor)
13 Death
14 The Devil
15 The Tower (The House of the Devil)

16 Hope
17 Prudence
18 Faith   *Salamandre*
19 Charity
20 Fire

21 Water
22 Earth
23 Air
24 Libra
25 Virgo
26 Scorpio
27 Aries
28 Capricorn
29 Sagittarius
30 Cancer
31 Pisces
32 Aquarius
33 Leo
34 Taurus   *Rossi*
35 Gemini

The Star
The Moon
The Sun   *Arie*
The World
The Angel

The last eight cards (*Rossi* and *Arie*) all have red backgrounds. The last five (*Arie*) are unnumbered.

None of the Minchiate cards bear printed names. The names given above are translations of names given in books or taken from similar cards in the other types of pack. There is some argument about the titles of the first five.

The trumps numbered 16 to 35 are the twenty trumps which are found only in the Minchiate series and which do not correspond to cards in the other types of pack. It will be seen that if these twenty are disregarded then the order of the remaining twenty is similar to that of the Charles VI type, omitting *The Popess* and transposing cards 9 and 10.

The Visconti Serpent
(Ace of Coins — late 15c.)

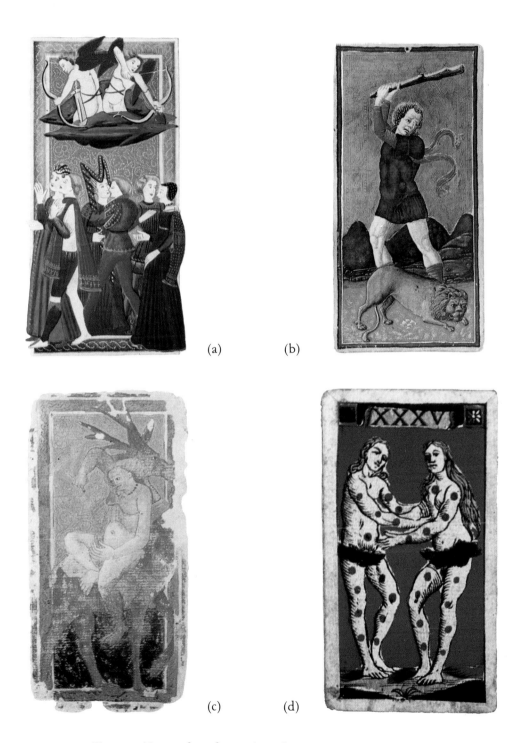

Figure 1. Trumps from four early packs:
(a) LOVE, from the Charles VI pack (15c.)
(b) FORTITUDE, from the Visconti-Sforza pack (15c.)
(c) TEMPERANCE, from the Catania pack (15c.)
(d) GEMINI, from a Minchiate pack (18c.)

(a)   (b)

(c)   (d)

Figure 2. Trumps from the Charles VI pack (15c.)
(a) TEMPERANCE
(b) FORTITUDE
(c) JUSTICE
(d) THE WORLD

PART 1

The Structure of the Trumps

Chapter 1

The Playing-card
Background

Playing-cards seem to have first appeared in Europe around the 1370s. The evidence for this is partly of the negative kind that no really clear reference to them before that time has been found. They do not seem to have been mentioned earlier in books or letters, nor in public records or other documents. The first positive and really reliable evidence of their existence in Europe appears to be a decree of the city of Florence of 23 March 1377, forbidding a game of cards which had been recently introduced there. But from then on there is a rapidly increasing amount of documentary evidence to show that the fashion for cards spread quickly. By the end of the century they were known in most of the larger towns of western Europe.

Where they had come from is not altogether clear, but the most likely thing is that they had been introduced into Italy from the Middle East. Cards had been invented some centuries earlier in China, which was the first country to make paper. From there they might have been brought along the trade routes, perhaps by way of India and Egypt, to Venice. But their immediate source remains uncertain.

A fifteenth-century manuscript, said to have been copied from one originally written in 1377 by a German monk, describes a pack as having fifty-two cards, in four suits each having three court cards and ten pip cards.

Even in the early days the composition of the pack varied a little from one European country to another. The court cards were of varying kinds and numbers, and the suit marks also varied. In Italy the suits were usually Batons, Cups, Swords and Coins; in Germany, Hearts, Bells, Leaves and Acorns; and other suit marks were adopted in other countries.

Allowing for regional differences like these, however, the earliest European packs seem to have had a structure broadly like that of the ordinary 52-card bridge pack of the present day. There is no sign at all that any of the very early packs included the extra suit of trump cards which is the special characteristic of the tarot pack.

Exactly when tarot cards first came into use is, like so much else in the early history of cards, uncertain. An entry in the books of the Este court at Ferrara for 1442 refers to *carticelle da trionfi,* as tarot cards were called at first, mentioning the painting of the cups, the swords, the coins, the batons and all the figures of four packs. From the absence of further explanation it seems likely that they were already well known by then, and on this one might make a guess of around 1440 for their invention. Various earlier dates have been put forward from time to time, but for one reason or another these all look doubtful or suspect, often because it is not clear that the references were to tarots rather than other kinds of playing-cards.

The art historian Robert Klein looked at a number of attempts to establish the dates of existing packs of early tarot cards from contemporary documents. He came to the conclusion that effectively there was no reliable documentary evidence for the date of any of the earliest surviving tarot packs; for their dating one could only look at the style of the cards themselves.

What are probably the earliest existing tarot cards are three hand-painted packs thought to date from around 1445, often called the 'Bembo' cards after Bonifacio Bembo, of Cremona, who is generally believed to have painted them.

Though these three packs have all been in other hands for many centuries, there seems no doubt that they were originally made for the Visconti-Sforza family of Milan. They bear in their designs the heraldic devices of the Visconti, lords of Milan in the fourteenth and fifteenth centuries, and of their successors the Sforza. The Visconti motto 'A bon droyt' ('With Justice') has been worked into the pattern of many of the pip cards in these packs.

These early 'Bembo' cards are of a magnificence never afterwards equalled. Hand-painted with great care and illuminated in gold and silver, they are a good deal larger than the cards we are accustomed to today. Their size, some 7 by 3½ inches (173 × 87mm) and the thickness of the card on which they are painted, has sometimes raised the question whether they were ever intended for actual play. From their obvious costliness, at a time when relatively cheap ways of making ordinary playing-cards by woodcuts and stencils were already becoming known, it has been suggested that they might have been intended as prestige wedding presents, or perhaps for gifts on special occasions rather like the famous Fabergé easter eggs in Imperial Russia. Be that as it may, they are beautifully made. Cards from one of these 'Bembo' packs are illustrated in Figures 3 and 4. Further illustrations will be found in Kaplan, pp.65-98, and in Part 2 of the present book.

Besides the three 'Bembo' packs, quite a number of other examples of early handpainted tarot cards still survive, including some more cards bearing the devices of the Visconti-Sforza. Some of these too may possibly have come from Bembo's workshop in Cremona, perhaps made by his assistants.

Others, including a set bearing the arms of the Este family (Kaplan, pp.117-8), and the so-called Charles VI cards (Figure 2, and Kaplan, pp.112-116) probably came from Ferrara.

Ferrara was known for its skilled miniature painters, producing finely illuminated manuscripts. It soon gained a reputation also for making playing-cards of particularly good quality, at first hand-painted, later woodcut-printed and handcoloured or stencilled. Apart from the Visconti-Sforza cards perhaps from the region of Milan, Ferrara was the most important centre for the production of tarot cards during the early period.

Sometime in the second half of the fifteenth century woodcut-printed tarot cards began to appear, though it is difficult to put an exact date on this because so few examples are known. The more elaborate and costly handpainted cards would have been treated as works of art and have consequently been much more carefully preserved than the plainer sets of cards which would have been simply thrown away when worn out and have rarely survived. There may well have been quite a long transitional period during which elaborate hand-painted cards were still being made for the ducal courts and so on, while cheap woodcut cards were already in use in the home.

By the first half of the sixteenth century however the large majority of tarot cards were woodcuts or occasionally copper engravings. The game of tarot had spread to other countries, in particular to France, but it is probable that Italy remained the most important source of production of the cards for a while.

While the ordinary 52-card pack may originally have been introduced into Italy from the Middle East, there is nothing at all to suggest an eastern origin for the tarot pack. Many of the trumps, such as *The Pope* and *Judgement,* could hardly have originated outside Christian Europe; here again all the indications point to Italy.

In all the existing early tarot packs in which a substantial number of cards have survived, the trumps are always found in company with minor cards — court cards or pip cards — and never on their own. The surviving cards may be mostly trumps, as in the Charles VI set where there is only one other card, a court card; or there may be numerous minor cards with only two or three trumps, as in one of the three 'Bembo' packs. The early record from Ferrara already mentioned, also refers to the painting of the suit cards and all the figures of the *trionfi* packs. There is no sign at all that the trumps ever existed as a separate pack on their own without court or pip cards, as has sometimes been suggested.

In a manuscript volume of sermons written in northern Italy in the latter half of the fifteenth century by a preaching friar one of the sermons deals with games of chance, which he divides into three kinds, dice, cards, and triumphs. This shows once again that in the early period the usual name for the tarot trumps was triumphs (Italian *trionfi* or Latin *triumphi,* from which the English word trumps was derived). It was not until rather later that the Italian word *tarocchi* and its French equivalent *tarot* came into use.

Our friar regarded the game of triumphs as particularly odious to God, bringing in as it did not only God himself, the angels, the planets and the cardinal virtues, but also the lights of this world, *The Pope* and *The Emperor.* He says that the pack consists of twenty-one triumphs, twenty-one steps on the ladder leading down to Hell; which seems incidentally to confirm the tradition that *The Fool* is to be regarded as a separate trump. He went on to give a list of the trumps, which shows that by his time the composition of the pack was already basically the same as we know it today.

To a few of the titles of the cards in his list he has added brief comments which are sometimes interesting. Thus after *The Chariot* he had added the note *'vel mundus parvus'* ('or the little world', i.e. the microcosm, man); while after *The World* he gives the alternative title *'cioe dio padre'* ('that is, God the Father'). Extracts from the sermon were published in 1900 in *Archaeologia,* vol. 57, by

Robert Steele, and it will be referred to here as the 'Steele' sermon.

From an early date then, the tarot already contained the full twenty-one trumps with which we are familiar today; but it is possible that this might not have been true of all the very early packs. Of the three 'Bembo' packs of around 1445, all are incomplete to some extent, so that it cannot be said with absolute certainty exactly how many cards they originally contained; at least one of these packs had some trumps which differ from the familiar ones, while another contains six trumps apparently of rather later date, so that its original composition may have undergone some modification.

The sequential order, too, of the earliest packs seems to have differed from the order which later became widely accepted as standard. The main types of order have been listed in the Introduction to this book. The whole question of order will be discussed more fully later, but for the moment it can be said that there may have been a development period of up to perhaps fifty years or so after the original invention of tarot cards before the pack arrived at the kind of composition and order which will here be called the 'standard' order. Even then, older types of order continued in use. Michael Dummett's *The Game of Tarot* is a mine of information on these points, as too is Stuart Kaplan's *The Encyclopedia of Tarot* which contains many illustrations of cards which cannot easily be found elsewhere.

To sum up what has been said here, it seems that the tarot pack was invented in Italy, probably around 1440, and was the result of an extra suit of trump cards having been added to the ordinary 52-card pack of court and pip cards which had already been in use in Europe since about the 1370s. (At some point extra court cards had also been added.) What are probably the earliest surviving tarot cards, the three 'Bembo' packs, are thought to date from around 1445, though it may not have been until rather later in that century that there came into use what I have called the standard order.

Chapter 2

Ways of Approach

Everything we know of the background of the age in which the tarot trumps came into being suggests that there is likely to have been some kind of systematic plan underlying them. As C. S. Lewis has put it, medieval man was not a dreamer, he was an organizer, a codifier, a builder of systems. Renaissance Italy inherited to the full the medieval traditions of systemized thought.

Against such a background the tarot trumps can hardly have been a mere jumble of rather quaint pictures, an untidy ragbag of images. They were designed to serve in games of cards which, by their nature, were based on the principles of hierarchy, with cards of higher rank taking precedence in some way over those of lower standing. The ordinary 52-card pack had reflected a social structure of the simplest kind. The tarot trumps show us a more elaborate picture of the universe, from the human situation up to the Last Things, and they must have been arranged in an order which reflected the following in some way of the hierarchical system of their universe.

That we do not, at first sight, immediately perceive the formal pattern underlying them does not necessarily mean that this was based on occult teaching or hidden wisdom. It may be simply that our whole outlook on the world has changed since then, and that what looks strange and disordered to us today would have seemed plain and straightforward in the fifteenth century.

The question is then how we should set about looking for the underlying system on which the trumps are arranged?

There are, broadly, two ways of approach. Either we can look at the cards themselves, trying to see some kind of plan in their order. Or we can look at the ambience in which the tarot was born, to see what kind of ideas were in the air at the time and which might be reflected in the trumps.

It might be thought that the first of these ways, looking at the cards themselves for their plan, would be likely to yield the clearer and more positive results. But in practice the thing is not so simple. The trumps take us into the world of symbolism, and it is in the nature of symbolism that it can be interpreted in many ways and at many levels of meaning. It is all too easy to read into the cards the teaching of some arcane school of thought. And an enormous variety of sources for the tarot have been suggested at one time or another. To name a few, Albigensian, alchemical, astrological, biblical, gnostic, hermetic, kabalistic, magical, Manichaean, Mithraic, Neoplatonic, numerological and Sufist origins have all been put forward. And it may well be that some of these have in fact influenced the symbolism of the trumps, as they have contributed something to the whole culture of the western world.

But however illuminating such interpretations may sometimes have seemed to be, they have not yet provided any really satisfactory answer to the problem of the scheme of the tarot as a whole. Far from helping to reveal its ground plan they have often obscured it by introducing concepts and systems that are rather unlikely to have been in the minds of the fifteenth-century Italian designers.

The second way of approach, looking as a control at the cultural background of the period in which the tarot was invented, can help us by eliminating at the start many of the hairier schemes, even though it may take us into some unfamiliar and rather strange fields.

We need in fact to use both ways of approach, first standing back a little and looking to see what kinds of ideas were in fashion at the time and then moving nearer and taking a closer look to see whether we find the same ideas in the tarot trumps. There is however a parallel field of art which will be of the very greatest help to us in this — the art of the engraved print.

Both playing-cards and prints are concerned with the making of multiple copies of a graphic image, and it is no accident that cards and prints both came to have a hold on man's interest at much the same time and in much the same places. So long as cards had to be individually hand-painted, the cost of an elaborate series like the tarot trumps would prevent them from ever becoming really popular. The development of the techniques of woodcut and engraving was essential for the spread of the tarot.

Where prints take the form of a set they often carry with them something of the same idea which we find in playing-cards, the idea of a hierarchical series. This affinity between packs of cards and sets of prints is thus often both close and fundamental.

The making of prints on paper had started with woodcuts. The later technique of using engraved metal plates was invented in northern Europe in the earlier part of the fifteenth century, but it seems that it was not until about 1460 that it reached Italy.

In Italy the art of engraving was thus developing at much the same time as the tarot also was in its developmental stage, and we can usefully look at the very earliest Italian engravings — particularly when these form a set or series — for insight into the kinds of ideas and ways of thinking that are likely to have influenced the designers of the tarot.

There are in fact three series of early Italian engravings which are outstandingly helpful. These are the sets of six prints known as the Triumphs of Petrarch, the sets of fifty prints often called the Tarocchi of Mantegna, and the sets of seven prints usually called the Children of the Planets.

The earliest examples of all three of these series date from around 1465, or only a very few years either side of that date. At that time there were still only very few engravers at work in Italy and the number of prints being produced there was still quite small. The greater part of their output was of religious subjects — annunciations, crucifixions, martyrdoms and so on — and if we leave these out of account the three series discussed here probably represented quite a substantial part of the total production of secular sets of prints made in Italy before, say, 1470.

Given the ready market for religious subjects, the engravers would not have spent the fairly considerable amount of time involved in making these secular series unless they were reasonably confident that they would sell well. The fact that it was thought worthwhile to produce them suggests that the subjects were already well known and consequently likely to have immediate appeal to the buying public. We can thus use the prints as indications of some of the kinds of ideas that were in the air at the time.

It will not be possible to illustrate here more than a few of these prints. There is however an outstandingly important standard work of reference in this field. This is *Early Italian Engraving* (7 volumes, London, 1938-48) by A. M. Hind, a former Keeper of Prints and Drawings in the British Museum. Besides being a most valuable source of information it contains excellent reproductions of all the sets of prints discussed here, and references to 'Hind' should be understood to mean this work.

Before going on to discuss these three series of prints in detail it will be useful first to take a look at the two most important surviving packs of early tarot cards.

Chapter 3

The Charles VI Pack

There are quite a number of early hand-painted tarot cards in the museums and art collections of the world. Many of them are either single cards or very incomplete sets having only a few of the trumps, and these do not offer much help towards understanding the structure and composition of the tarot pack. The sets which are important to us are obviously those which contain a substantial number of the trumps.

There are two early packs which are of particular interest in this way because they show nearly complete sets of the trumps. These are one of the three 'Bembo' packs mentioned in Chapter 1, and the set usually called the 'Charles VI' pack.

With a few variations, the designs of the cards in both these two packs are for the most part recognizably much the same as in say the present-day Marseille pattern. Both packs are hand-painted. In neither of them do the trump cards bear numerals as an integral part of their designs, and because of this there has been some uncertainty about their proper order.

First, to discuss the so-called Charles VI cards. This pack, now in the Bibliothèque Nationale in Paris, has seventeen surviving cards; fifteen of these are trumps, and there is also a *Fool;* the remaining card is a court card, the Page of Swords. Some reproductions are illustrated in Figures 1 and 2. Illustrations of

all seventeen of the originals will be found in Kaplan, pp.112-116.

The cards are hand-painted and illuminated in gold and silver, though with not quite the delicacy of style and artistic attractiveness of the 'Bembo' cards. Like those, they are of fairly large size, some 7 by 3¾ inches (180 × 95mm).

The story went that they were painted for the amusement of Charles VI of France, in the first of his periodic fits of madness.

In 1704 some extracts from the royal household accounts were published by Père C. F. Menestrier, which showed that in 1392 a payment had been made to one Jacquemin Gringonneur, painter, for three packs of cards for the king. As no earlier references to cards were then known, Menestrier suggested that the painter had specially invented them to amuse the king in his illness, and that this represented the origin of all playing-cards.

Later on, the idea was put forward that these seventeen tarot cards must be the remains of one of the three packs painted by Gringonneur for Charles VI.

In point of fact there is really no connection at all between the seventeen tarot cards and the record in the royal household accounts. There is no evidence even to show that the cards painted by Gringonneur were tarots; probably they were ordinary playing cards. In any case it is now accepted that the seventeen tarot cards, though of considerable age, are a good deal later than 1392 and of North Italian, rather than French, origin. One of the most authoritative writers on early cards, the late W. L. Schreiber, considered that they perhaps came from Ferrara. They are thought to date from the second half of the fifteenth century.

However the old story of their having been painted for Charles VI still turns up regularly in books on the tarot, and as the cards are so well known by that name they will be called here the Charles VI pack.

First, there is the question of the sequential order of the trumps. It has already been mentioned that the early hand-painted cards did not carry numerals in their designs. In the case of the Charles VI pack however there are in fact some small hand-written numbers in the top margins of the cards (not shown in the reproductions illustrated here). These are roman numerals, written in pen-and-ink. The handwriting is considered to be not later than the first half of the sixteenth century, but there is nothing to show that they were written at the actual time of painting of the cards. The pen-and-ink looks a little out of place on cards carefully illuminated in gold and silver, and it seems rather unlikely that the painter himself would have written the numbers on the cards in this way, in ordinary handwriting. All one can say is that the numbers were written on the cards at an early date by someone who may or may not have known the intentions of the designer but thought that this was the right order.

The numbering on the Charles VI cards is given in the Introduction. The highest number in these hand-written numerals is twenty. It is conceivable that the pack might have had no more than twenty trumps plus the unnumbered *Fool,* but it has been shown by Michael Dummett that the numbering in this type of order seems often to have started with the second lowest trump rather than with the first. This would mean that *The Magician* (which is missing from the Charles VI pack) could have been treated as a second unnumbered card, and this would reconcile

the numbering (twenty plus *The Magician* and *The Fool*) with the usual total of twenty-one plus *The Fool.*

The whole problem of the order of the trumps has been admirably discussed by Michael Dummett in his book *The Game of Tarot,* and a much fuller exposition of the matter will be found there.

For our purposes here however the important thing is that the numerals on the Charles VI cards seem to give one of the types of order in use at an early date. Though the Charles VI cards themselves are to be dated as later fifteenth century, there is no reason to think that this pack was a prototype, and the order which they give may well have been in use at an earlier date. It will in fact be shown later that this was probably the original order of the trumps when invented around 1440.

There are various differences between this order and the type usually regarded today as standard — see the tables in the Introduction — but the most important one is that the three Cardinal Virtues, *Temperance, Fortitude* and *Justice,* are found together as a group (6, 7, 8) immediately after *Love* (5), instead of being split up as in the standard order, where they are 14, 11 and 8 respectively.

The second point which comes up here is what I call Group Coding. By this I mean the use in early hand-painted packs of some symbol or special similarity of treatment to indicate an internal group amongst the trumps, often though not always consecutive cards, but always cards having something in common with each other. It may have been used in this way only in one particular pack, and great caution is needed in making comparisons of this kind between different packs, as the designers may have had quite different ideas on the minor details of the symbolism. The principle is of particular value when looking at a single pack, individually painted by one or perhaps two hands. It is no longer of much help with later cards, when the designs had settled down into conventional stereotypes often of widely mixed ancestry.

In the Charles VI pack there is a particularly

clear example of Group Coding in the three Cardinal Virtues, *Temperance, Fortitude* and *Justice,* who are shown neatly outfitted in uniform style with haloes of a polygonal kind often worn by the ladies of their profession.

Given the highly systematic nature of the programmes used by artists in the fifteenth century, it seems most unlikely that only three of the traditional four Cardinal Virtues should have been represented in the tarot. To find the missing fourth Cardinal Virtue, Prudence, we have to look for another lady dressed in the same way. A fourth lady wearing a polygonal halo is to be found later in this pack, where she is standing on top of *The World.* In the mind of the designer of the Charles VI cards she was fairly clearly meant to have been taken as Prudence, often regarded as the highest of the Cardinal Virtues. The four cards are shown in Figure 2. It must be emphasized that this identification is not necessarily to be applied

to other kinds of pack.

Another example of Group Coding in the Charles VI pack lies in the use of blue sky or blue clouds to represent Heaven. This is found in *Judgement (The Angel), The World, The Sun* and *The Moon,* and would almost certainly have been shown in *The Star,* which is missing from the pack — five cards concerned with Heaven.

Standing apart from the main group of five cards but as a kind of pendant to it, blue sky has also been used in one other card in the Charles VI pack, *Love.* Here it is clearly meant to signify love coming down to man and woman on Earth as a special gift from Heaven, the gift of the cosmic life force. The card is shown in Figure 1.

The concept of Group Coding will prove of great help in unravelling the sequence and structure of the next pack to be considered, the Visconti-Sforza set.

Chapter 4

The Visconti-Sforza Pack

This is one of the three splendid packs believed to have been painted by Bonifacio Bembo of Cremona (though it has to be said, in passing, that the attribution to him has not been established beyond all possible doubt). It contains seventy-four cards, only four short of the standard seventy-eight. The four lacking cards, which were almost certainly present at one time, are *The Devil* and *The Tower*, and two of the suit cards. It thus has nineteen out of the standard twenty-one trumps, as well as *The Fool*; they are unnumbered. Some are illustrated in Figures 1, 3 and 4.

The two missing trumps may perhaps have been deliberately destroyed by someone who thought it wicked to play cards with *The Devil*. And *The Tower* was often represented as a hell-mouth, a way down to Hell.

The cards of this hand-painted pack bear many Visconti and Sforza heraldic devices in their designs, and there seems no doubt that they were originally made for one of the members of the Visconti-Sforza family. While there are quite a number of other surviving hand-painted cards bearing Visconti-Sforza devices, this set is by far the most nearly complete, and it will be called here the Visconti-Sforza pack.

It is now in divided ownership, part being in the Pierpont Morgan Library in New York, part in the Accademia Carrara in Bergamo,

Italy, and part being held by the Colleoni family also of Bergamo, but until the nineteenth century all the cards were together as one set. Facsimile reproductions in colour in the form of a pack of cards have been produced by Grafica Gutenberg of Bergamo in co-operation with U.S. Games Systems, Inc., of New York. Black-and-white illustrations can be found in Kaplan, pp.65-86, and in Part 2 of the present book.

The Visconti had been lords of Milan since the middle of the fourteenth century. Filippo Maria Visconti became third duke of Milan in 1412. In 1441 his daughter Bianca Maria Visconti married Francesco Sforza, who had already been given the right to use the name Visconti. Filippo Maria died in 1447, and after an interval Francesco became fourth duke of Milan in 1450.

The balance of probability seems to lie rather in favour of the pack having been made for Filippo Maria Visconti, who incidentally is known to have been very fond of playing games of various kinds.

There is no direct evidence to show the exact date at which it was painted, but there is an interesting bit of indirect evidence in a manuscript (Cod.Pal.556) in the Biblioteca Nazionale in Florence. This is a story-book about the adventures of some of the Knights of the Round Table of Arthurian legend, particularly Tristram, Lancelot and Perceval. It contains a large number of pen-and-ink illustrations more or less integral with the text and which must have been made at much the same time as that was written. A note at the end of the manuscript says that it was handed over on 20 July 1446.

It is generally accepted that these pen-and-ink drawings are by the same hand as some of the trumps of the 'Bembo' packs.

In one instance some parts of the figures in cards of the Visconti-Sforza pack are so closely similar to those in one of the pen-and-ink drawings in the manuscript that it looks almost as though one had been copied directly from the other.

It seems reasonable to think then that the Visconti-Sforza pack, which was probably the latest of the three packs attributed to Bembo, must have been painted in the main very near to 1446 — the date given in the manuscript — perhaps within a year or so.

There is however another problem here, one which is of crucial importance. While most of the cards of the Visconti-Sforza pack thus seem to have been painted around 1446, there are six trumps in the pack which have clearly been painted by some other hand and which appear to be of a rather later date.

These six trumps by the later hand, which will be called here the 'new' cards, are *Fortitude, Temperance, The Star, The Moon, The Sun* and *The World*.

It is noticeable that none of these six new cards contain any of the Visconti-Sforza devices found in the older cards of the pack, suggesting that at the time when the new cards were painted the ownership of the pack might already have passed out of the immediate circle of the Visconti-Sforza of Milan, perhaps by way of a marriage gift for example. The style of the new cards is thought to be that of the miniature painting schools of Ferrara. Robert Klein considered that they dated from around 1480-1490, which would put them some forty years or so later than the main part of the pack.

The question arises why these six new cards should have been made. It has sometimes been suggested that they were replacements for cards that had become worn or lost, but this looks rather unlikely. The condition of the other cards in the pack is fairly good and does not suggest great carelessness of use. Moreover the artistic style of the six new trumps is quite distinctive and they cannot possibly have been intended as exact copies of older cards, as might have been expected for worn or missing ones.

The most likely explanation seems to be that there was some kind of reorganization of the Visconti-Sforza pack and that the purpose of the new cards was to convert it from an older form (perhaps, for example, of Charles VI type of order) into the new kind of sequence which eventually came to be accepted as standard. In its new form the Visconti-Sforza pack would thus have been a precursor of what has come to be called the Marseille type.

The new cards of the pack contain several instances of Group Coding which support this. The most important and the most elegant of these is a group of three of the new cards, *The Moon, The Star* and *Temperance.* Here the three ladies wear dresses of classical style, sufficiently similar to suggest that they were meant to form a group, but with their individual attributes carefully distinguished. (Figure 3.)

The question we are meant to ask is why the three ladies were dressed in this way. The answer is that they were dressed in classical style because they had been given parts in a classical myth.

The key is that in the myth the moon was a triple goddess. Lemprière's *Classical Dictionary,* under *Hecate,* tells us that she was called Luna in Heaven, Diana on Earth, and Hecate or Proserpine in Hell, whence her name of *Diva triformis.*

Offerings were to be made to her especially on highways and at crossroads, and she was given the name of *Trivia,* goddess of the three ways leading to Heaven, the Earth and sea, and Hell, the three regions to which her power extended.

In the Visconti-Sforza pack as *The Moon,* Luna, she is shown holding her crescent aloft, up towards Heaven. Her dress, the blue of the

Hecate. (Causei, *Museum Romanum*, vol. i. tav. 21.)

sky, is covered by a robe of violet-purple patterned with the triple golden rays of the sun whose light she reflects. Here she is the Queen of Heaven.

As *The Star*, Proserpine, she wears a reversible cape of red and green, the red to symbolize the Earth parched by the sun during the summer months when she is away in the Underworld with her husband Pluto *(The Devil)*, the green to symbolize the fertility which comes back to the Earth with the moisture she brings when she returns (her blue dress is patterned with stylized rainclouds). She is the Queen of Hell, the Venus of the Underworld.

As *Temperance*, Diana or Ceres or the Great Mother, she is the power of the moon on Earth. She pours the spirit of life from Heaven down to Earth, from one vessel to another. Her blue dress is patterned with the stars of Heaven to show that she is of celestial birth, a goddess, even though she wanders on Earth in human form searching for her daughter, Proserpine, abducted by Pluto.

The scheme bears all the marks of Renaissance humanism, where meticulously worked out programmes drawn from classical sources would be furnished to artists for their paintings of mythological subjects. It has to be

remembered that in fifteenth-century Italy the normal language in school was Latin, and people were far more familiar with the Latin poets, especially Ovid and Virgil, and through them with classical myth, than we are today. Mythological allusions in art, such as the Triple Goddess, would have been quickly recognized and appreciated.

The theme of tne Triple Goddess had to be worked into the Visconti-Sforza pack in such a way that, as Trivia, goddess of the three ways, she would command the three roads leading to Heaven, Hell and Earth. This meant that *Temperance* (Ceres) had to occupy a position in the pack where she would still form a fairly tight group with the other two, *The Star* (Proserpine) and *The Moon* (Luna).

In both the Charles VI and Steele types of order *Temperance* occupies a much lower place in the pack, at number 6 in the sequence, or thereabouts. It seems then that the Visconti-Sforza pack, at least in its form with the new cards, must have followed the standard type of order, in which *Temperance* is number 14. (See Table 1.)

There is a further instance of Group Coding in the Visconti-Sforza pack, in the use of a red foreground in some cards. In the shape of low red cliffs, this is found in five of the six new cards: *Temperance, The Star, The Moon, The Sun* and *The World*. Only *Fortitude*, of the new cards, does not have it.

Two of the older cards also show red foreground: *Death*, again in the form of the low red cliffs, and *Judgement*, in a rather different form. Another of the older cards, *Love*, has been given an overall red background. There are thus a total of eight 'red' cards (Figures 3 and 4.)

In the Charles VI pack blue sky had been used to denote Heaven. In much the same way, in the Visconti-Sforza pack the red ground has been used to show immortality.

The red symbolizes the sphere of Fire, the middle region between Earth and Heaven in medieval cosmology. In the Proserpine myth Ceres had bathed a child in fire, to give it immortality. When the dying Cleopatra feels her soul beginning to leave her body and rise

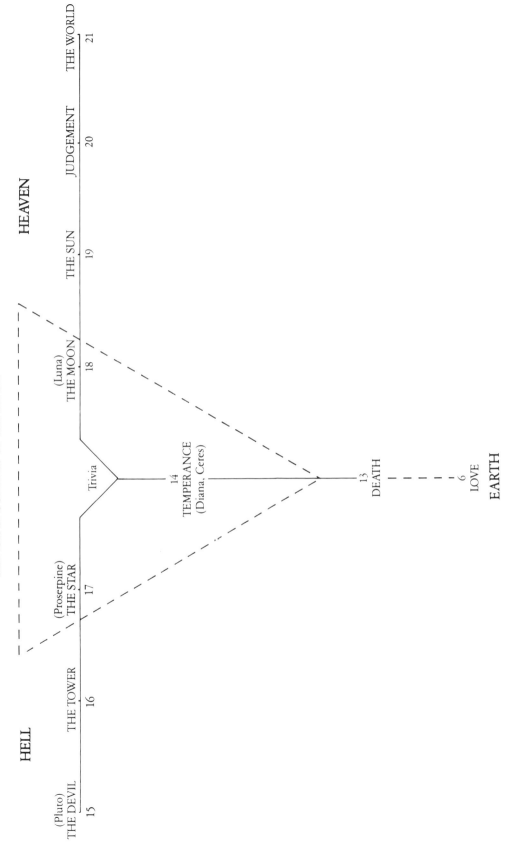

Table 1. The Chain of Generation.

upward to Heaven, Shakespeare has her say: 'I have immortal longings in me . . . I am fire and air; my other elements I give to baser life'.

To have passed upward through the sphere of Fire was to have gained immortality, to have shed the body and its lower elements. In the Visconti-Sforza pack the figures who have passed through the sphere of Fire, who now stand *above* the red ground, are immortals.

The main sequence of the red cards starts with *Death,* which can be regarded as the gate into eternal life. *The Devil* and *The Tower* are both missing from the pack but as they represented Hell rather than Heaven it seems unlikely that they would have been granted the red carpet treatment. The series of red cards then continues to *The World,* the Heavenly City, the summit and end of the pack.

It is noticeable that *Fortitude* (Figure 1), alone of the six new cards, does not show a red foreground. The card shows Hercules slaying the Nemean lion, the first of his labours. Originally Hercules was not an immortal. He had been born of a mortal mother and it was only after his death, in fire, that he was received into the company of the gods and granted immortality. Here, with no red foreground, he must have figured in the tarot story before *Death,* before gaining immortality.

Fortitude, which does not have the red ground, must thus have ranked lower in the pack than *Temperance,* which has it. This relative placing of the two is found only in the standard order, confirming that the Visconti-Sforza pack must have followed that type of order, in which *Temperance* is number 14.

The remaining red card is *Love.* As with the blue sky cards of the Charles VI pack, so too in the red cards of the Visconti-Sforza pack *Love* is the only card of the group to be far separated from its main sequence, to which it seems again to form a kind of pendant. The symbolism is of love as bringing with it the kind of immortality that can be achieved while still on Earth, through the continuity of human generation and the racial immortality that can overcome personal mortality.

Love has been given an overall red background; it is the only one of the trumps which does not have a background of gold. I think it was given this special treatment to mark it as one of the keys to the whole sequence. It is to be noted that the red is here a background, not a foreground. The lovers are still on Earth. They have not yet passed upward through the sphere of Fire; they are still mortals.

In medieval allegory love carried an even wider range of meanings than it does today. It meant human love, both physical and emotional. It meant divine love, the love of man for God and the love of God for man, love as the essence of the nature of God expressed in the creation. But love was also the fundamental power of attraction, the power of cohesion which kept the four elements from falling apart in discord and chaos and which caused the spheres to follow their orderly paths in the heavens. Love was the cosmic life-force, the power behind the working of the universe.

The singling out of *Love* as a key card in the Visconti-Sforza pack reflects this medieval concept of love as the great motive force of the whole cosmos.

Besides their symbolic significance, the red cards may also have served a more practical purpose in card games. A look at the Minchiate pack shows a rather striking parallel. Once again there are eight 'red' cards, the three *Rossi* and the five *Arie,* all of which show red grounds (see list in the Introduction, and Figure 1).

While not all the red cards in the Minchiate correspond exactly to those in the Visconti-Sforza pack, there is sufficient similarity between the two series to make it most unlikely that the occurrence of eight red cards in each was a pure chance coincidence. The inventor of the Minchiate must have known of the eight red cards in the Visconti-Sforza pack and must have taken over the broad idea, though with the variation that he found it more convenient for his purpose to provide a straight run of eight red cards at the end of his pack. Besides a special significance in scoring,

Figure 3. Trumps from the Visconti-Sforza pack (15c.)
The Triple Goddess: THE MOON, THE STAR, TEMPERANCE.

Figure 4. Trumps from the Visconti-Sforza pack (15c.)
The other five 'red' cards: LOVE, DEATH, THE SUN, JUDGEMENT, THE WORLD

in this position they may perhaps also have indicated a shortened form of pack for games in which the full number of trumps would have been too cumbersome.

But the essential point is a simpler one: the existence of the group of eight red cards in the Minchiate offers strong support for the eight red cards in the Visconti-Sforza pack also having been meant to form a group.

We can now see the outlines of the story told by the Visconti-Sforza cards. Look again at Table 1. (p.31).

The whole cosmos was to be regarded as moved by love, working at many levels, through the divine creation and through generation.

In Heaven *The Sun* and *The Moon* are the Lord and the Lady of Generation, ministers carrying out God's plan for the creation, through love. They are not Time itself but they cause Time to pass and they mark its passage through the passing of the seasons and the hours.

Beyond *The Sun,* in Eternity, beyond all thought of Time, lies the Resurrection and *Judgement* at the Last Day. Then the faithful shall come to a new *World,* the City of God, the New Jerusalem. (In a minor instance of Group Coding, the use of angels or cherubs in these last three cards reminds us that here we are in the empyrean, the Heaven of the Trinity and of God the Father).

The Sun, the Lord of Generation lies next to his Lady and twin sister, *The Moon.* But love is needed to bring them together, and in Heaven this is brought by Venus herself, as Proserpine, *The Star,* when she returns each year from the Underworld with her moisture.

When Pluto, *The Devil,* had abducted Proserpine he had taken her down to his kingdom. *The Tower* is the hell-mouth through which she has to pass between Earth and Hell and Heaven.

Her mother Ceres, *Temperance,* had wandered all over the Earth looking for her and had abandoned her duty as the Great Mother, causing the Earth to become desolate and infertile, a barren place. With the return of Proserpine with her moisture, Ceres can once again resume her duty, and fertility will come back to the Earth.

The Triple Goddess, *The Moon, The Star,* and *Temperance,* provides the links between the worlds. Though appearing on Earth, Ceres is an immortal, a goddess; she bridges the crucial gap between Heaven and Earth. As *Temperance,* with her perpetual cycle of regeneration she brings transcendence of *Death,* through love. But hers is love on the scale of universal Nature, the Earth Mother, rather than at the level of the individual.

It is through the son of Venus, Cupid, *Love,* that the final stage in the plan of generation is brought into play, and man and woman and all physical forms of life are given individual existence on Earth. And it is through *Love* too that mankind can begin the re-ascent to Heaven.

In the shape given to the pack by the new cards, the Visconti-Sforza set seems to have been a direct ancestor of all tarot packs which follow the standard order, perhaps best known in the form of the Marseille pattern. But before looking further at its structure it will be useful to take a look at the earliest form of the tarot story.

Chapter 5

The Original Story

One of the fascinations of the tarot is the feeling it leaves that there is a hidden meaning of some kind lying in the order in which the trumps appear.

Taken one by one, the images of the trumps can all be found in other fields of medieval art. They were not newly invented for the cards. The designers used images and symbols which, like *The Wheel of Fortune,* were perfectly familiar at the time and which would not in themselves have seemed mysterious.

Perhaps it is a natural habit of the human mind to try to see a pattern in things. But just as a strip cartoon has no meaning without a story to connect the pictures, one feels that the order of the tarot trumps must have followed a story or a plan of some kind. Particularly since the trumps did not at first carry numbers in their designs, there must have been something which served to link together all the separate cards and made their sequence seem a right and proper one.

The meaning of the pack need not of course be restricted for ever to only one story. Once devised, the trumps of the tarot pack would provide an alphabet of symbols as it were, which could be rearranged to spell out variations in the story, or even completely different stories. The different types of order which have been in use at one time or another imply that changes in the story did occur.

An outline of the story apparently underlying the Visconti-Sforza pack has been sketched in the last chapter. But the new cards in that pack suggest that some kind of reorganization had in fact already taken place, so that the story in it may originally have been a different one.

If we can find the theme of the story originally underlying the tarot it will be easier to understand both the original order of the trumps and the original reasons for the choice of the images which went to make up the pack. It will also be easier to see the reasons for the changes of order which took place later.

We can here take up a suggestion put forward by Gertrude Moakley, that the tarot was originally based on the Triumphs of Petrarch.

Around 1340 the Italian poet Petrarch had written a poem celebrating the conquests of Cupid over gods and men; this he called the Triumph of Love. In it the poet tells of a vision in which he sees Cupid on a fiery triumphal chariot, followed by an immense procession of lovers, the victims and captives of Cupid through the ages, in history, in story, in myth.

A friend steps out from the procession and joins the poet, to tell him the names of the famous as they pass.

At last Laura appears and, captivated by her, the poet himself joins the procession as yet one more victim of Cupid.

To the Triumph of Love, Petrarch soon added the Triumph of Chastity, in which Cupid is defeated by the power of chaste love personified in Laura and her Virtues. After a struggle Chastity takes Cupid prisoner and leads him captive in her own triumphal procession.

The identity of the real Laura is not entirely certain but she is thought to have been a Laura de Noves, who married Hugues de Sade by whom she was to have eleven children. Perhaps Petrarch was simply following the conventions of courtly love with all its obligatory frustrations and repinings, or maybe Laura found his rather copious love poems a bit much, but anyway she seems to have kept Petrarch at a certain distance. Whoever she was, the real Laura died in 1348, and he then wrote the Triumph of Death. In this he tells of her willing acceptance of fate and her serene death witnessed by a great company of the dead as well as by her still living friends.

Over the years he added further Triumphs to the poem. In the Triumph of Fame he relates a vision in which Fame triumphs over Death; the poet sees a long procession of those who by their deeds in life have gained the fame which lasts beyond death and gives a kind of immortality.

Continuing the pattern in which each Triumph is undone by the following one, there next came the Triumph of Time, in which Fame, the last of human vanities, is in turn conquered by Time and oblivion; the Sun had speeded up his motion so as to make Time pass more quickly.

In the last of the Triumphs, the Triumph of Eternity, written in 1374 the year of his death, Petrarch relates a vision of a new world, changeless and everlasting, in which even Time will be overcome, by Eternity; and at the Last Day he will be reunited with Laura, in Heaven.

In the next two centuries the Triumphs of Petrarch achieved immense popularity. It was accepted right from the start that the poem was a moral allegory of the stages of life and of the states of the soul, in life, death and resurrection. It circulated widely in manuscript, and a large number of copies are known. Enormously long and learned commentaries on it were written.

The manuscripts soon began to carry illustrations, and the theme of the Triumphs spread also into other fields of art. There are many examples of engravings and woodcuts, paintings, decorated furniture, pottery and enamel, tapestries, and so on. As Hind put it, no theme outside the stories of scripture gave more frequent employment to artists and craftsmen of the fifteenth and sixteenth centuries.

In 1956 Gertrude Moakley, writing in the *Bulletin of The New York Public Library* (vol. 60, no. 2) drew attention to the very close parallels between the tarot trumps and Petrarch's poem, a comparison which she subsequently elaborated in an interesting book.

To summarize very briefly the main points put forward in her paper, there are two valuable clues to the origin of the tarot trumps: their Italian name *trionfi,* and the original absence of curiosity about the meaning of the cards, showing that it must have been taken for granted. Petrarch's *I Trionfi* not only has the same name as the tarot trumps, which were called *trionfi* at first, but it was a poem so universally familiar in the courtly circles in which the early hand-painted tarot cards were to be found, that the cards would have been immediately recognized as alluding to the poem. A comparison of the many illustrations of Petrarch's *I Trionfi* with the tarot trumps shows that both do in fact tell something like the same story. Moreover it was for the Visconti family, who had been patrons of Petrarch, that the 'Bembo' cards were painted.

To this we may add that the time at which tarot cards seem to have been invented coincides closely with a period of increasing interest in the theme of the poem in pictorial art. In the splendid catalogue, *Early Italian Engravings,* produced by the National Gallery of Art in Washington for an exhibition in 1973, the comment is made that the

Triumphs of Petrarch were a favourite subject in book illumination from the 1440s and onward, and of considerable importance in other decorative arts.

The making of a pack of cards based on the Triumphs would have been an entirely natural development. It is in fact from just that time — 1442 — that we have the first documentary record of the painting of tarot cards — at Ferrara, which was a centre of book illumination.

The circumstantial case for this origin for the tarot trumps is thus strong.

Gertrude Moakley went on to suggest how the twenty-one trumps should be allocated to represent the six Triumphs. It was here that her thesis ran into difficulties. While one can agree with many of the allocations which she proposed there were several which did not fit well.

In her original paper she had used the standard order of the trumps (the Marseille order) as the basis for her comparison. In her subsequent book she changed to the use of the Steele order, but this still left difficulties.

However, only one small modification is needed. This consists of taking into consideration the point made by Michael Dummett, already mentioned in Chapter 3, that in packs of the Charles VI type the numbering of the trumps seems often to have begun with the second lowest trump, rather than with the first.

If we adopt the Charles VI order with this point in mind, the trumps fall into place as illustrations of the Triumphs perfectly smoothly and without difficulty of any kind.

The Fool can be regarded as representing the poet himself, or as Everyman. *The Magician* then becomes another unnumbered card representing the friend and guide who in the poem steps out of the procession and joins the poet, telling him the names of those who were passing in it; he is the master of ceremonies of the vision.

The remaining trumps then fall neatly into four sets of five cards each, without further adjustment of any kind. The first three of these sets of five represent the Triumphs of

Love, Chastity, and Death. The final set of five combines the three Triumphs which come after death, those of Fame, Time and Eternity, which in some ways are less suitable for expanded pictorial treatment. In decorative art too the first three Triumphs were used as subjects more frequently than the last three.

The scheme also fits the Steele order very well, though with the difference that it is then the final card, *The World,* which has to be taken as the further unnumbered card standing outside the main series, instead of *The Magician.* There is some evidence to support this in an uncut sheet of cards, probably of the late 1400s, in the Metropolitan Museum of Art, New York. This sheet broadly follows the Steele type of order, and in it *The World* is definitely left unnumbered, though numbers appear on all the other trumps. (Dummett, plate 5).

The list of trumps given in the Steele sermon itself (Kaplan, p.xvi, 2, 3) tells us that *The World* could be taken as God the Father. I think the Steele order was a later variant of the Charles VI type, invented by someone with a nice sense of theological decorum who felt that the final trump in the pack, representing God the Father as the First Cause, ought not to be lumped into a group with other cards but should stand outside the main series, in a class of his own as it were.

It would have been with this aim that *Justice* (Astraea) was promoted to the penultimate position in the Steele order, there probably representing the return of the Golden Age foretold by Virgil in his *Eclogue IV,* which was very well known in medieval times and regarded as a kind of pre-Christian messianic prophecy. *Justice* would then form a group of five cards with *Judgement, The Sun, The Moon,* and *The Star.* This would allow *The World* (God the Father, symbolized by the new world, the City of God, the New Jerusalem) to be treated as the final trump, standing on its own outside the rest of the series.

Whether taken in the Charles VI or in the Steele order, the trumps fit the Triumphs of Petrarch so well, and the circumstantial case is so strong, that it seems difficult not to accept this origin for the tarot. It is worth emphasizing that Petrarch was immensely well known in Italy in his own time; indeed he was one of the most widely known literary figures in the whole of Europe.

Before leaving the Triumphs a glance at the Minchiate will again be helpful.

The Minchiate type of pack was invented in Florence sometime around the early 1500s. It was apparently constructed by adding a further twenty trumps to the already existing 21-trump type, omitting one trump of the latter, so as to bring the total to forty trumps plus *The Fool*.

Michael Dummett has pointed out that since the twenty additional trumps in the Minchiate have been inserted at a certain

The Triumphs of Petrarch and the Tarot Trumps

Charles VI Order	The Onlookers	Steele Order
The Fool	The poet himself. Everyman.	The Fool
The Magician	The poet's friend and guide.	
	THE TRIUMPH OF LOVE (the life of the senses)	
1. The Popess		1. The Magician
2. The Empress	The triumphal procession of Cupid,	2. The Empress
3. The Emperor	with his captives.	3. The Emperor
4. The Pope		4. The Popess
5. Love [Cupid in triumph]		5. The Pope
	THE TRIUMPH OF CHASTITY (the life of virtue)	
6. Temperance		6. Temperance
7. Fortitude	The triumphal procession of	7. Love [Cupid now captive]
8. Justice	Chastity. Laura in the	8. The Chariot
9. The Chariot	Chariot, while Fortune, soon	9. Fortitude
10. The Wheel of Fortune	to turn, still shines on her.	10. The Wheel of Fortune
	THE TRIUMPH OF DEATH	
11. The Hermit (The Old Man)	Faith and wisdom, but approaching Death.	11. The Hermit (The Old Man)
12. The Hanged Man (The Traitor)	Fate and destiny, but hope of redemption.	12. The Hanged Man (The Traitor)
13. Death	Death.	13. Death
14. The Devil	Satan the tempter.	14. The Devil
15. The Tower	Hell.	15. The Tower
	THE TRIUMPHS OF FAME, TIME, ETERNITY	
16. The Star	Fame. The Star of Bethlehem.	16. The Star
17. The Moon	Clock time. Sublunar time.	17. The Moon
18. The Sun	The controller of Time. Cosmic time.	18. The Sun
19. The World	The poet's vision of the world to come.	
20. Judgement (The Angel)	The Last Judgement.	19. Judgement (The Angel)
	Justice on the Last Day. Return of the Golden Age.	20. Justice
	God the Father, or the First Cause. The City of God. The New Jerusalem.	21. The World

Figure 5. The Triumph of Love
Woodcut from an early edition of Petrarch's *Triumphi* (Venice, 1488).

point in the sequence of standard trump subjects as a consecutive block (numbers 16 to 35) of new cards, we can remove them and study the resulting order in reasonable confidence that it represents an order in use at the time the Minchiate pack was invented. In fact, the resulting order is almost identical with the Charles VI type.

What is especially interesting to us here is the precise point at which the twenty new trumps were inserted into the sequence. Their insertion immediately after trump number 15 has been made at exactly the point at which it would best give recognition to and least disturb the structure of the older cards, if those were a pack of the kind we have envisaged, broadly of Charles VI type and representing the Triumphs of Petrarch. The insertion at that point would in effect keep intact the first three sets of five cards (numbers 1 to 15) representing the Triumphs of Love, Chastity, and Death, and the introduction there of the twenty additional trumps (of theological and cosmological subjects) would place these in the natural position to lead up to the final set of five cards culminating in the Last Things, taken over from the older series.

This underlines the point that the structure of the Charles VI type of pack seems to have been based on four main groups of five cards each, and further strengthens the case for the tarot having been originally founded on the Triumphs.

One more point concerns the actual designs of the Minchiate cards. These remained exceptionally stable over the centuries and so it is likely that the twenty cards in the Minchiate taken over from older types of pack will preserve types of designs already in use in the Florence area at the time when the Minchiate was invented. For this reason it is particularly interesting to see that some of the Minchiate designs seem to fit the story of the Triumphs especially well.

For example, in the Minchiate designs, *The Star* shows one of the Wise Men from the East, under the Star of Bethlehem, which seems a much more fitting illustration of Fame than

the lady in the new Visconti-Sforza card. *The Moon* includes a clockface, bringing out more clearly the connection of the card with the Triumph of Time. *The Sun* shows a pair of lovers who might well represent Petrarch united with Laura at the end of Time (Kaplan, p.52).

This strengthens the likelihood that one of the reasons for the new cards in the Visconti-Sforza pack was to replace designs of an older kind (broadly like those preserved in the Minchiate), which had been perfectly appropriate in a pack intended as illustrations of the Triumphs of Petrarch but which were no longer suitable when the Visconti-Sforza pack was reorganized on a different plan and with a different story.

As might be expected from the already well established popularity of the theme, the Triumphs of Petrarch were one of the earliest secular subjects to be taken up after the art of engraving had reached Italy around 1460. Reproductions of a set of six prints of the Triumphs dating from about 1465 will be found in Hind, and also a second set dating from a few years later. There were many subsequent editions.

There was a good deal of variety in the ways the poems were translated by artists into pictures. The two prints illustrated here, while not the earliest, have been chosen for their special appositeness to the tarot.

The first of these, The Triumph of Love (Figure 5), is a woodcut book illustration from a 1488 printed edition of the poem. It shows two onlookers in the background, clearly the friend or guide telling the poet the names of those who were passing in the procession of captives. Tied to the triumphal car is a figure like *The Fool* — Everyman after he has been captured by Cupid. In the foreground is *The Popess* with her book.

The second illustration, The Triumph of Death (Figure 6), is a rather later engraving (c.1540) by a German artist, Georg Pencz. After Death has mown with his scythe souls divide into two streams, one of which goes between a ruined Tower and the jaws of Leviathan, down into the fires of Hell. The

NASCENTES·MORIMVR·FINISQZ·AB·ORIGINE·PENDET· ·
LONGIVS·AVT·PROPIVS·MORS·SVA·QVENOZ·MANET· ·

Figure 6. The Triumph of Death   Engraving by Georg Pencz (c.1540)

other stream leads upward towards the Sun and then to a domain in the clouds, Heaven.

It may well have been a matter of common knowledge amongst miniature painters and book illustrators in the fifteenth century that *trionfi* cards had originally been based on Petrarch's *I Trionfi,* and one may think that an artist commissioned to produce a new set of prints of the Triumphs might have taken a look at the tarot trumps to see what ideas he could pick up. The two prints illustrated here may in effect show some reflex influence from the tarot in this way, but in any case they underline the close similarities between the poem and the cards.

Tarot cards then, invented around 1440, seem originally to have been based on the Triumphs of Petrarch and at first to have followed the Charles VI type of order or something close to that.

The three 'Bembo' packs all appear to date from about the 1440s and it thus seems likely that they would all originally have followed, broadly, the Charles VI type of order.

In what was probably the earliest of the three, the so-called Visconti di Modrone set, there are three trumps not found in other tarot packs (though appearing in the Minchiate), the three Theological Virtues,

Charity, Faith and Hope. It seems the most economical supposition that in the Visconti di Modrone pack these three cards had appeared together as a consecutive group after the three Cardinal Virtues, possibly separated from those by *The Chariot,* but being replaced in the later two 'Bembo' packs by *The Wheel of Fortune, The Hermit,* and *The Hanged Man,* respectively. However the pack is too incomplete to be certain of this, particularly as the cards are not numbered.

The second 'Bembo' pack, the so-called Brambilla set, has only two surviving trumps, so that little can be said of it, though one of these is *The Wheel of Fortune,* which is at least not inconsistent with what has been suggested above.

The third 'Bembo' pack, the Visconti-Sforza set, was probably originally of Charles VI type but as discussed in the last chapter it seems to have been modified at a later date so as to follow the order which eventually became standard and was the ancestor of the Marseille and similar types of pack.

We can now leave the Triumphs of Petrarch and turn to look at some other series of early prints, to see what help they can give us with the tarot story.

Chapter 6

The Three Worlds

The fundamental principle of a pack of playing-cards is the rule of hierarchy, with cards of higher value taking precedence over those of lower standing. So long as we are dealing with sequences like the ordinary 52-card bridge pack, with its four suits of court cards and pip cards, this does not raise any problem. But when we come to the tarot pack with its twenty-one trumps which did not at first carry numbering and even when later given numbers are still found in varying kinds of order, things become more complicated and difficult to understand.

There is however a series of prints which can give us a great deal of help over the way the principles of the hierarchy of the universe were understood in the fifteenth century.

The so-called Tarocchi of Mantegna are a series of fifty copper engravings, rather like the early tarot trumps in general style but only occasionally the same as the trumps in actual subject.

For the series as a whole Hind adopted the title of 'The Governance of the World'. As he observed, the prints seem designed to form a compendium of instruction in the medieval view of the universe, with its systematic classification of the powers of Heaven and Earth.

Small drawings of the whole series are shown in Figure 7. Larger reproductions of four of the prints appear in Figures 8a and 10.

Reproductions of the whole series and a good deal of background information will be found in Hind, and they are also described in Kaplan, pp.37-47. A set of reproductions in the form of a pack of cards was issued by Edizioni del Solleone of Milan in 1981.

The prints are of much the same large size as early tarot cards, though usually left uncoloured. They are on thin paper. No set of original impressions mounted on card for playing has ever been found, but on the other hand there are several examples of the entire series bound as a volume and some of these bindings seem to go back to the period of the original publication of the prints. They appear to have been intended for use in book form for instructive purposes rather than as a pack of playing-cards; they may have served as the key for some kind of memory game, or for meditation.

There are two early Italian editions of the fifty prints. The first edition can be dated, within two or three years or so, as being around 1465. A second edition, mostly fairly close copies of the first edition though often reversed, dates from a few years later.

At one time they were thought to have been by Andrea Mantegna. The attribution to him was dropped many years ago but they are still so often called the Tarocchi of Mantegna that the name will be kept here. They are clearly of Italian origin and more recently

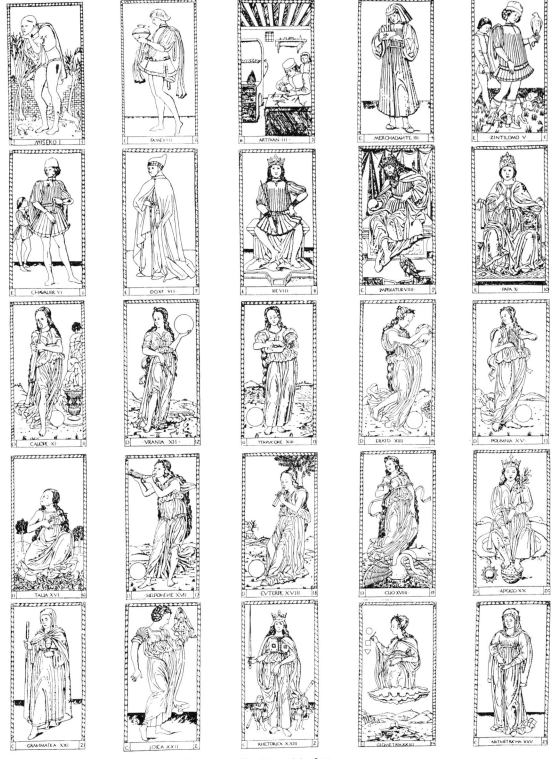

Figure 7. The Tarocchi of Mantegna
The fifty prints (c.1465)

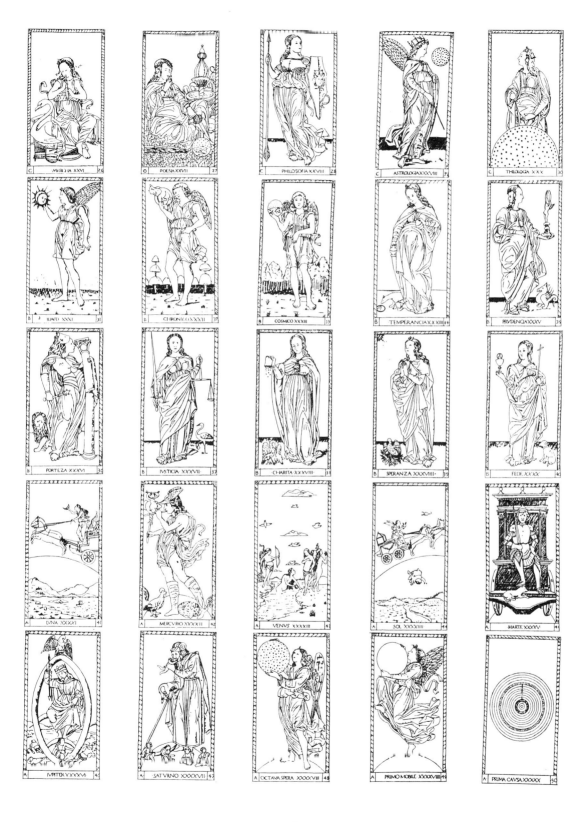

their attribution to the school of Ferrara has become accepted because of very close resemblances of style to the astrological frescoes of the Palazzo Schifanoia at Ferrara, known to have been painted around 1470.

Their date of around 1465 and their association with Ferrara thus place the Mantegna Tarocchi in the same ambience as early tarot cards, and indeed looking at the two side by side one can hardly avoid the impression of some connection between them, though the resemblance is more one of family likeness than of similarity in detail. The probable explanation is that the Mantegna series was planned by someone familiar with early tarot cards who deliberately adopted the general idea of the trumps for a set of instructive prints using the broad principles of a pack of cards, though only rarely using the actual subjects of the tarot. The use of cards for educational purposes of course became quite common later on.

It is not unlikely that the Mantegna Tarocchi, themselves influenced by early tarot cards, may in turn have influenced the later development of the tarot. For our immediate purpose here however the point is simply that as an instructive series the Mantegna prints are likely to reflect the kind of ideas about the hierarchy of the universe that were being taught in schools in Italy around the period when the tarot was still in its developmental stages — the ideas of hierarchy that were part of the whole world picture of the time and which we might well find reflected also in the tarot trumps.

The Mantegna Tarocchi is constructed of five sets of ten prints. Each print bears at its foot a letter identifying its set (in the first edition E, D, C, B, A), a title in Italian, and a consecutive number (1 to 50). English versions of the titles of the prints are given in the adjoining list. The class names given here to each of the five sets do not appear in the prints; they have been added for ease of reference only.

The subjects are largely traditional and, like the tarot trumps when taken individually, can mostly be found in other fields of art — in books, illuminated manuscripts, paintings,

sculpture in churches and so on. The real problem for us is not so much the source of ideas for the individual prints but, rather, the plan underlying the series as a whole.

The key to the basic structure is given by the last print of the series, the First Cause (Figure 8a). This is a sort of model or schematic diagram of the hierarchy of the universe, of a kind not uncommon in those days. A broadly similar diagram from a sixteenth-century book, though with some minor differences in some of the circles, is shown for comparison in Figure 8b.

The hub of the cosmological wheel is formed by four inner concentric circles representing the spheres of Earth, Water, Air and Fire, the four elements of the sublunar world, the mingling and mixture of whose qualities determined the natures of everything in the regions below the sphere of the moon. The elements should not be regarded as identical with their counterparts in the physical world but rather as symbolizing the essential principles underlying terrestrial earth, terrestrial water and so on.

The innermost of the four circles in the Mantegna diagram shows the sphere of Earth. This corresponds to the first set of prints, E, the Ranks of Man, in which all the figures are purely human, from the Beggar up to the Pope. This is the world of human personality, the world of everyday life on Earth.

The next circle in the diagram shows the sphere of Water. This corresponds to the second set of prints, D, figures of the Muses and Apollo. The Muses brought the arts to mankind; they stirred the artistic emotions in man and woman. They were believed to live on Earth around springs and streams, particularly the Castalian spring on the slopes of Mount Parnassus. They were nymphs, spirits of Water.

The third circle shows the sphere of Air and corresponds to the third set, C, of the prints, allegorical figures of the seven Liberal Arts and the three great wisdom disciplines of Philosophy, Astrology and Theology. Instruction and teaching of all kinds were thought to have affinity with the element of Air.

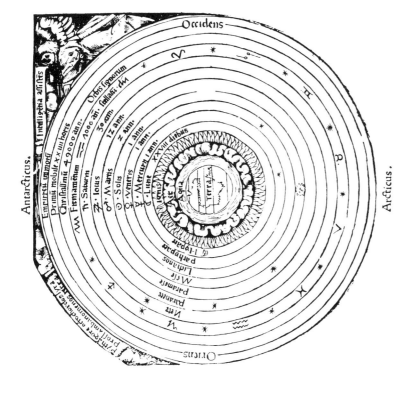

(a) From the Tarocchi of Mantegna: The First Cause (c. 1465). The division between the two innermost spheres, those of Earth and Water, is not very clear, perhaps intentionally.

(b) From Aristotle: Libri de Caelo, Ed. J.Eck, (Augsburg, 1519). The two innermost spheres, Earth and Water, here represent the terraqueous globe.

8. The Cosmos

The Tarocchi of Mantegna

Set E (the Ranks of Man)

 1 The Beggar
 2 The Servant
 3 The Artisan
 4 The Merchant
 5 The Gentleman
 6 The Knight
 7 The Doge
 8 The King
 9 The Emperor
10 The Pope

Set D (the Muses and Apollo)

11 Calliope
12 Urania
13 Terpsichore
14 Erato
15 Polyhymnia
16 Thalia
17 Melpomene
18 Euterpe
19 Clio
20 Apollo

Set C (the Liberal Arts and the Sciences)

21 Grammar
22 Logic
23 Rhetoric
24 Geometry
25 Arithmetic
26 Music
27 Poetry
28 Philosophy
29 Astrology
30 Theology

Set B (Angels and Virtues)

31 Iliaco
32 Chronico
33 Cosmico
34 Temperance
35 Prudence
36 Fortitude
37 Justice
38 Charity
39 Hope
40 Faith

Set A (the Heavens)

41 Moon
42 Mercury
43 Venus
44 Sun
45 Mars
46 Jupiter
47 Saturn
48 Eighth Sphere, the Zodiac
    and Fixed Stars
49 Primum Mobile, the First
    Moving Sphere
50 Prima Causa, the First Cause,
    the Unmoved Mover

The fourth circle shows the sphere of Fire and corresponds to the fourth set of the prints, B, in which all the figures are of angelic nature: Iliaco, Chronico, Cosmico and the four Cardinal Virtues and the three Theological Virtues. The sphere of Fire, highest and most rarified of the four sublunar elements, was the home of the angels, the messenger spirits who had form but no physical bodies. They could cross the lunar boundary which divided the celestial regions from those below; they could rise to Heaven but they could also descend to Earth. The soul, which shared in the nature of both Heaven and Earth, was regarded as having affinity in many ways with the sphere of Fire.

The four innermost circles in the cosmic diagram thus represented the spheres of the four elements of the sublunar world and corresponded to the first four sets of the Mantegna prints. Around them and encompassing them come the circles of the spheres of the Heavens, the celestial and divine worlds, shown in the final set, A, of the prints. In this set are the seven planets of antiquity, the eighth sphere of the zodiac and the fixed stars, and the ninth sphere of the Primum Mobile, the First Moving Sphere which sets in motion the rotation of the heavens and the rising of all the stars and planets.

Finally comes the First Cause, represented in our diagram by three further circles the outermost of which is fringed with sunlike radiance spreading out to infinity; these stand for the Trinity — the Holy Spirit, Christ the King of Heaven, and God the Father — they may also carry a more humanistic interpretation along neoplatonic lines.

The first four sets of the prints had represented the spheres of the four elements of the sublunar world. This final set, A, the celestial and divine worlds, must correspond to the fifth of the classical elements, Aether, the divine element which was believed to fill the heavens above the moon. Macrobius for example, in his *Commentary on the Dream of Scipio*, (1,xxi,33), widely read in medieval times, had put it like this: 'But from the

highest realm down to the moon all things are holy, imperishable and divine, because in them is that aether which is always the same and never stirred by mutability.' This fits the fifth set of our prints exactly, in which the highest realm is that of the First Cause (print A 50), showing the empyrean Heaven of the Trinity, and the lowest is the Moon (A 41).

The five sets, A, B, C, D, E, may be regarded as the successive stages in the Creation and also as levels in the descent of the soul through ever more dense states of being, down to the terrestrial world, the world of the senses. The numbering of the prints, 1 to 50, in reverse order to the sequence of the lettering of the sets, would then represent the steps up through the hierarchy of existence, the steps on the ladder by which the soul may reascend from Earth up to Heaven, through the Ranks of Man, through the cultivation of the Muses, through learning the Liberal Arts and practising the Virtues, and finally through the powers of the planetary gods up to the realm of the First Cause, there to be reunited with the Divine Spirit.

The five elements formed the whole of the universe. Of these however Earth and Water were of heavy nature, whose natural movement was downward. Air and Fire on the other hand were light elements, whose natural movement was upward. (Compare the speech of dying Cleopatra, already quoted on page 32.)

The four elements of the sublunar world thus tended to separate out into two groups, Water sinking down to the level of Earth to form the terraqueous globe on which we live, while Air rose upward to coalesce with Fire. Only Aether remained immutable. The result was a cosmos of three worlds, with the sphere of Fire forming a middle world between Heaven and Earth.

It is this sphere of Fire which is symbolized in the Visconti-Sforza pack by the red ground; to rise above it is to gain immortality. Fire could be regarded as allowing Spirit to pass from Heaven down to Earth — the tongues of Fire which were symbols of the descent of divine power; Fire could also burn and consume material things, turning Earth into Spirit, the reverse movement as it were. Fire thus formed a middle term, a middle world in the chain of being between the aethereal world of Heaven and the mundane world of Earth.

Ptolemy, in the *Tetrabiblos* (Book 1, Chapter 2, Ashmand's translation) had expressed it like this:

> That a certain power, derived from the aethereal nature, is diffused over and pervades the whole atmosphere of the earth, is clearly evident to all men. Fire and air, the first of the sublunary elements, are encompassed and altered by the motions of the aether. These elements in their turn encompass all inferior matter, and vary it as they themselves are varied; acting on earth and water, on plants and animals.

This division of the universe into a hierarchy of the elements may be seen in an illustration from Konrad von Megenberg's *Buch der natur* (Figure 9a), the structure of which corresponds broadly to the diagram in our Mantegna print of the First Cause.

The same thing may be seen in more pictorial form in an illustration from Sebastian Münster's *Cosmographia* (Figure 9b). These illustrations bring us very close to the world of the tarot.

The doctrine of the three worlds took many forms, but in one shape or another it was accepted by almost everyone. It was not an occult teaching. It was simply part of the general explanation of how the universe worked, the world mechanism.

In the microcosm, Man, the three worlds found their correspondence in body, soul and spirit. The soul was a little chopped-off bit of spirit as it were, whose descent from Heaven gave Life to the body for a while and whose eventual withdrawal was Death. Hell and Purgatory could be added to the teaching according to taste.

If we look at the tarot in this light, it is in fact the doctrine of the three worlds which seems to provide the basic frame of order of the trumps in the standard sequence.

In the Charles VI type of order and its

modified version the Steele type, which had both been based on the Triumphs of Petrarch, the cards fell into four main groups of five cards each, with an extra card outside the main groups. In the new type of sequence which eventually came to be regarded as the standard order, the trumps now seem to fall into three sets of seven cards.

The most important difference between the two lies in the position of *Temperance*. In the Charles VI and Steele types *Temperance* had been given an early position in the pack, where she had taken a prominent part in the Triumph of Chastity. In the new standard order she has been moved up considerably so that she now becomes number 14. In this position she completes a second set of seven cards which includes all the Virtues.

The cause of her promotion was that she had now taken on the role of one of the three forms of the Triple Goddess. As the Earth Mother, the terrestrial form of the Moon Goddess, here at the end of the second set she acts as the crucial link between Heaven and Earth, between Eternity and the worlds of Time, pouring the eternal spirit down into an unending succession of temporal forms.

The first of the three sets of seven in the new standard type of tarot sequence consists of figures which are purely human. It represents activities in the terrestrial world of everyday life, the world of human personality. It corresponds broadly to set E of the Mantegna series, the Ranks of Man, which also includes an *Emperor* and a *Pope*. I call this set the Realm of Man.

The second set consists of figures all of which are allegorical. It deals with the spirit in man, the soul from its entrance into the human body at birth to give it the power of movement *(The Chariot)* which is life, until its withdrawal in *Death*. It includes all the Virtues, being completed by *Temperance*. The set corresponds broadly to set B of the Mantegna series, the Angels and Virtues. I call it the Realm of the Soul.

The third set consists of figures of a theological or celestial nature. It shows the life beyond *Death,* with *The Devil* and *The Tower*

(b) from Sebastian Münster: *Cosmographia* (1550)

(a) from Konrad, von Megenberg: *Buch der natur* (1499)

9. The Cosmos

representing the fate of the imprudent soul consigned to Hell, while *Judgement* and *The World* show the Resurrection and the proper reward in Heaven for the virtuous. It corresponds broadly to set A of the Mantegna series, the Heavens. I call this set the Realm of Eternity.

A table comparing the Charles VI type with the standard order may help to make this clearer. In the standard order *The Hermit* has been shown here in both the first and the second set. In some ways he belongs to the first set, in other ways to the second; he overlaps the two.

He is one of the human figures in the trumps and in that sense he belongs to the first set, the Realm of Man, bringing its total up to seven; as *The Old Man* he is clearly the most senior member of the human group. But even making the utmost allowance for the fairly cynical atmosphere of Renaissance courts, where popes were often not greatly revered, it is also clear that he could not be placed immediately above *The Pope*, who must be given top place in the ranks of man, as in the Mantegna series.

The solution adopted in the standard order was to give *The Hermit*, though human, a place in the second set, the Realm of the Soul. Perhaps he was felt not to belong entirely to the world of man. But besides overcoming the tricky problem of social precedence this would allow him also to take over the part of Prudence, the missing Cardinal Virtue, whose

The Charles VI Order and the Standard Order Compared

	Charles VI order: The Triumphs of Petrarch		Standard order: The Three Worlds	
Everyman The guide	The Fool The Magician		The Fool	
The Triumph of Love (the life of the senses)	The Popess The Empress The Emperor The Pope Love	{	1. The Magician 2. The Popess 3. The Empress 4. The Emperor 5. The Pope The Hermit (The Old Man) 6. Love (The Lovers)	} The Realm of Man (human figures)
The Triumph of Chastity (the life of Virtue)	Temperance Fortitude Justice The Chariot The Wheel of Fortune	{	7. The Chariot 8. Justice 9. The Hermit (Prudence) 10. The Wheel of Fortune 11. Fortitude 12. The Hanged Man (The Traitor) 13. Death 14. Temperance	} The Realm of the Soul (allegorical figures)
The Triumph of Death	The Hermit (The Old Man) The Hanged Man (The Traitor) Death The Devil The Tower	{	 15. The Devil 16. The Tower	}
The Triumphs of Fame, Time, and Eternity (the life after Death)	The Star The Moon The Sun The World Judgement (The Angel)	{	17. The Star 18. The Moon 19. The Sun 20. Judgement 21. The World	The Realm of Eternity (figures of the afterlife)

role in the Charles VI order had been filled by *The World*.

The Hermit would thus have had a foot both in the Realm of Man and in the Realm of the Soul. The association of hermits with Prudence was traditional; and Prudence too had something of the same double nature, reflected in the way she is portrayed in the Mantegna series with two faces, one that of an Old Man looking backward as though to his worldly past *(Memoria),* the other that of a young woman like the Virtues, looking forward to the future life of the soul, and Eternity *(Providentia).* In the mirror of self-knowledge she sees things as they truly are *(Intelligentia).*

In early versions of the card *The Hermit* was shown holding an hourglass, symbolizing his original connection with the Triumph of Death. In later designs the hourglass was usually changed to a lantern. I think this change arose from *The Hermit* having taken over the role of Prudence. In one well-known medieval text Prudence had been called the lantern.

The tarot with only twenty-one trumps cannot be expected to correspond in detail to the fifty prints of the Mantegna series. But as has been seen there are broad parallels

between the two. Both are concerned with the hierarchy of the universe, a hierarchy based on the three worlds and finding expression in the tarot in what I have called the Realms of Man, of the Soul, and of Eternity.

The next chapter will show a further parallel between the two series.

Chapter 7

The Angels of Generation

Our look at the Tarocchi of Mantegna has shown the broad plan of that series and has suggested that the three worlds also form the basic frame of order of the standard tarot sequence, with the trumps falling into the three sets which I have called the Realms of Man, of the Soul, and of Eternity.

The key to the main structure of the Mantegna Tarocchi was given by the final print, the First Cause. But the prints also offer another key, now to the passageways which link together the three worlds. Again there is a broad similarity between the prints and the tarot, and again the prints will help us to see the structure of the tarot more clearly.

While the subjects of the Mantegna prints are for the most part familiar and orthodox ones, there are three figures which Hind says are not known to occur elsewhere in medieval or Renaissance art. These are Cosmico, Chronico and Iliaco (B 33, 32, 31), see Figure 10. Because they are unique, we may think that they were meant deliberately to invite attention.

They are based on terms used in medieval astronomy. In the classic astronomical text of the Middle Ages, the thirteenth-century treatise of Sacrobosco, *De sphaera,* it is said that the rising and setting of the signs according to the poets is threefold, cosmical, chronical and heliacal — *'cosmicus, cronicus et eliacus'.* Cosmico, Chronico and Iliaco are allegorical personifications of these three terms.

It is not easy, today, to understand the importance given in the Middle Ages to explanations of a figurative kind, in which physical and psychological forces were represented by allegorical personifications. The universe was felt to be fundamentally poetical in its nature, in a fashion that escaped and went beyond purely factual description. It was the poet who, by his art, could in some ways best capture the inmost nature of things. Poetry and allegory were accepted ways of explaining and understanding reality.

Taken separately, Cosmico, Chronico and Iliaco could be interpreted in a variety of ways. But when these three figures, unique in pictorial art, are found together as a group in the Mantegna prints and in that order, it becomes virtually certain that they were meant to carry an allegorical meaning related in some way to the kind of explanations given by Sacrobosco of the cosmical, chronical and heliacal risings of the stars.

The question that has to be asked, then, is why the risings of the stars should have been chosen as the pegs on which to hang an allegory?

The rising of the stars resulted from the rotation of the heavens. This was brought about by the Primum Mobile (A 49), the first moving sphere, shown in the Mantegna prints

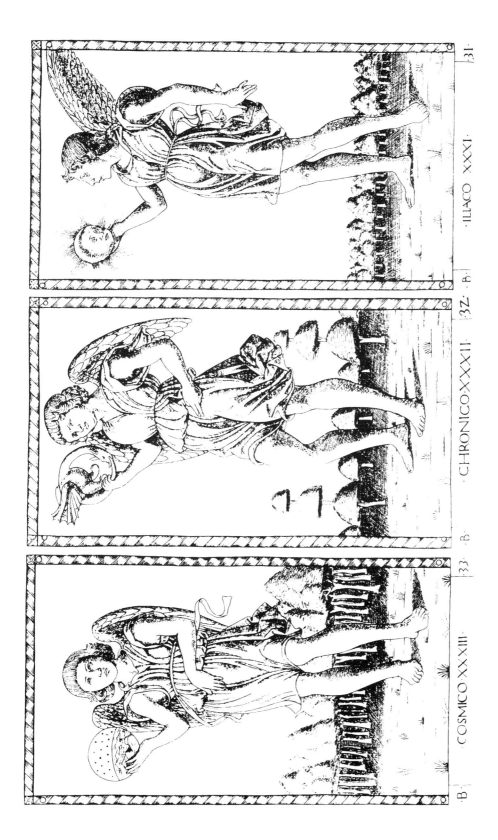

Figure 10. The Angels of Generation
From the Tarocchi of Mantegna (c.1465)

as an archangel playing with the globe of the cosmos; the Primum Mobile had been charged by the First Cause (A 50) with the duty of starting the cosmic dance. It was the impulse given by the Primum Mobile to the Eighth Sphere (A 48), the sphere of the zodiac and the fixed stars, which set going the rotation of the heavens and the emergence above the horizon of the stars.

The rising of the stars above the horizon was a symbol of coming into being, birth; the Latin word used by Sacrobosco for the rising of the stars, *ortus,* also signified beginning, origin. Their emergence from the cosmic womb, as it were, marked the birth of the signs of the zodiac and of the sun and the moon and the other planetary gods and led eventually to the creation of the sublunar world of mutability and finally of man. The first rising of the stars began the creation; its repetition each day brought about the continuance of the processes of birth and generation.

Cosmico, Chronico, and Iliaco, as personifications of the three kinds of rising of the stars, must then be connected with the creative and generative powers of the cosmos. Since they have been placed only in set B of the prints, below the Virtues, they cannot themselves be the primary generative powers; they must be, rather, the executive officials of those powers, their famuli if you like, genius figures. In the prints they have been given proper angel wings, and as angels, messengers or intermediaries between Heaven and Earth, we may regard them. I shall call them here the angels of generation.

As the officials in charge of the rising of the stars they would have had the duty of supervizing the processes of generation, looking after the imprinting of the proper forms on shapeless matter as this was brought above the horizon by the rotation of the heavens. The three angels are shown in the prints against backgrounds of trees because forests symbolized primal matter, the formlessness to which it was their job to give form and shape; the Latin word *silva* was used in medieval allegory to mean both forest and primordial matter.

To use another simile common in medieval times, their duty would have been to attend to generation by stamping the seals of form on the wax of matter.

There are three of them because they represent the different ways in which the powers of generation are manifested in the three worlds, and which were to be studied through the three wisdom disciplines shown in the three immediately adjoining prints, Theology (C 30), Astrology (C 29) and Philosophy (C 28): theology for knowledge of the working of the divine world of Eternity, astrology for understanding of the cycles of time and the effect of the planets on the world of the Soul, philosophy for the study of life in the everyday world of Man, the physical world.

Coming back to Sacrobosco, the further explanation he gives in *De sphaera* (cap. 3) is that cosmical or mundane rising is when the sign or star ascends above the horizon from the east by day. Chronical or temporal rising is when the sign or star emerges above the horizon from the east at night; it is called temporal because astronomical time begins with sunset. Heliacal or solar rising is when the sign or star becomes visible because the sun moves away from it, when previously it could not be seen because of the nearness of the sun.

It will be realized that this threefold classification of the kinds of rising of the stars depends ultimately on the sun and the moon. The rising is cosmical if it occurs by day, when the sun is above the horizon and rules the sky; chronical if by night, when the sun is below the horizon and the moon is the ruler; and heliacal if near sunrise, when day and night the kingdoms of sun and moon come briefly together.

The sun and the moon, then, symbolized the primary generative powers of the universe; Apollo and Diana, they were twin aspects of a single entity. They were the Lord and the Lady of Generation, the ministers appointed in the chain of being with those responsibilities (Figure 9). The processes of creation had been set going, at God's command, by the Primum Mobile. The sun and the moon, themselves responsible to the Primum Mobile, exercise their powers through their own servants, the angels of generation.

The angels of generation administer the generative powers of the sun and moon at three levels, in the world of divinity and eternity, in the temporal world of the perpetual cycles of Nature, and in the terrestrial world of individual man and woman; as servants of the sun and moon they can be regarded as passing their power from one down to another, from Heaven down to Earth. In effect the three angels thus provide the links between the three worlds, through the powers of generation; and these links are of the nature of sun and moon.

Though Cosmico, Chronico and Iliaco seem to be unique in using the threefold risings of the stars to give symbolic expression to the workings of the generative powers of the universe, personified figures of generation of other kinds are not at all rare in the allegorical poetry of the Middle Ages; many examples could be given. In philosophy too there are to be found figures broadly of such a nature; to use a medieval term, the angels might be regarded as administering the seminal reasons, the potentialities of generation originally implanted by God in living beings, at the creation. Strange as they may seem to us today, in the fifteenth century the three angels would have been understood.

The Tarocchi of Mantegna appear to have been drawn by an artist of the Ferrarese school, around 1465. The new cards of the Visconti-Sforza pack are thought to have been painted around 1480-1490, and these too seem to have been by an artist of the Ferrarese school. One may think that figures performing broadly the same duties as the Mantegna angels of generation might be found also in the Visconti-Sforza cards.

Look again at the three angels (Figure 10). Their designs have been planned with the utmost meticulousness. Cosmico is shown in front view, full face, because his sphere of duty is the whole of the cosmos. The globe he holds is the cosmic globe, the globe of the whole of Heaven and Earth — the globe which is shown also in the print of Poetry (C 27) the creative art ruled by Apollo and shown too in the print of Apollo himself (D 20), the sun god. Sacrobosco has told us that a cosmical rising is one which takes place by day. Then, the sky is ruled by the sun. Cosmico must administer the generative power of the sun at the divine or cosmic level.

In the shortened cosmology of the tarot, with only twenty-one trumps against the fifty prints of the Mantegna series, the duties of Cosmico, the angel of the sun, are performed by *The Sun* itself, as the Lord of Generation.

Chronico is shown in three-quarter view, because his sphere of duty is the world mediating between Heaven and Earth. The trees in the background have been given a curious threefold pattern, to proclaim that he stands in the middle of the three worlds, in the garden of Adonis. Sacrobosco has told us that a chronical or temporal rising is so called because astronomical time starts here, with sunset; and this is where Time has been brought into the allegory, in the perpetually repeated cycle of life and death, the realm above the terrestrial world of Iliaco but below the divine world of Cosmico. Chronico is shown holding the dragon of Time devouring its own tail. He is the angel who attends to the regenerative cycle of Nature; he looks after the generative powers at the generic level and through the species rather than through the individual. A chronical rising is one which takes place at night, so we may regard him as an angel of the moon.

In the tarot *Temperance* plays the same part as Chronico. In the standard order of the trumps she has been promoted to number 14. Here she completes the second set of seven cards, the Realm of the Soul, and links it through her participation in the Triple Goddess to the third set, the Realm of Eternity. Passing the spirit of life from one vessel into another, from one body to another, she is Nature, the Earth Mother, the power of the moon goddess on Earth.

Like Chronico, *Temperance* brings Time into the cosmic scheme, in her perpetually repeated cycle of life and death. The root of her name is related to *tempus,* time, as was well recognized in the fifteenth century when she was sometimes depicted with a clock on her head; a chronical rising would also be called a temporal one.

Iliaco is shown in side view, half face, because his sphere of duty is the terrestrial world, the lower half of the cosmic globe. His is the globe of the conjoined twins, sun and moon, the globe of Apollo in his form as the twin god.

A heliacal rising takes place at dawn; then, day and night the living kingdoms of sun and moon meet and join briefly together, in an act of love as it were, and the moon is fertilized by the sun. When the sun moves away along its path in the zodiac a star becomes clear of the sun's rays; so that a new star seems then to be born in the night sky. Iliaco, the angel of the heliacal rising, brings the generative power of the sun and moon, the twin god, down to man and woman, in physical love and birth.

In the tarot *Love* fills the same role as Iliaco. This is love at the human level, the love between man and woman which will create a new body and make it ready for the descent of the soul *(The Chariot)* which will give it life and movement. Here the part of the angel of generation is played by Cupid, always shown in the card and often represented as flying down from the sun. *Love* fulfils the same duties, at the level of the individual, as *Temperance,* concord, had done at the level of the species. The card forms the link between the first set, the Realm of Man, and the second set, the Realm of the Soul. In the Visconti-Sforza pack it had been marked as a key card by being given an overall red colouring.

A little more is needed here about Temperance, because of two rather different senses in which the word was used.

In one sense there is Temperance as a Cardinal Virtue. The parts of Temperance in this sense included moderation, chastity, continence, abstinence, sobriety and all manner of self-restraint; originally the lady in the tarot card had been mixing water with her wine. It was as a Virtue that Temperance

appeared in the Mantegna Tarocchi, and it was as a Virtue too that *Temperance* had appeared in the Charles VI type of order, where she had been given a place in the procession demonstrating in support of the Triumph of Chastity. In this sense of the word the emphasis is on the moral quality.

But Temperance could also be used in a rather different sense, as the physical action of mixing different elements so as to temper their qualities. In ancient and medieval cosmology the physical basis of creation had often been regarded as the tempering of the four elements, their being mixed together in due proportion, with finally the adding of the fifth element, aether, in the soul, to give life to the physical body.

In the first sense Temperance had figured from the microcosmic standpoint, as a moral striving in the individual soul, upward towards perfection. In the second sense she appears from the macrocosmic or cosmological point of view as a link in the downward chain of creation. Here she could be regarded as organizing and controlling the whole cycle of life and death, the cycle of perpetual regeneration.

By medieval times the various related Italian, French and English words seem often to have been used in both senses. Chaucer for example could use *Attemperance* for the moral Virtue of moderation, but he could also use the word in its cosmological sense. (*Boece,* book 4, metre 6):

> This attempraunce norysscheth and bryngeth forth alle thinges that brethith lif in this world, and thilke same attempraunce, ravysschynge, hideth and bynymeth [= takes away] and drencheth undir the laste deth, alle thinges iborn.

It was in this second sense, I think, that *Temperance* was now being used when she was moved up to her new place in the standard order. As one of the new cards in the Visconti-Sforza pack she is no longer merely the Cardinal Virtue she had been in the Charles VI order, she is now one of the three forms of the Triple Goddess.

Mixing together and tempering the elements, *Temperance* now holds the powers of Nature — not only life and not only death but also their perpetual recurrence. She is the regenerative power of the Earth Mother who gives manifestation in Time, like Chronico, to the generative powers of the moon.

In a few French and Belgian tarot packs the card was given the title of *Atrempance*, instead of *Temperance*, probably to reflect this wider sense which it now carried. (Kaplan, pp.135, 152. Dummett, plate 31.)

An early hand-painted tarot card in the Museo Civico in Catania, Sicily, depicts a naked girl on a stag (Figure 1). The condition of the paint makes some of the detail unclear, but it has been suggested by Stefano Bottari that the girl is pouring from one vase into another and should be identified as *Temperance*. The stag was an attribute of Diana because of the myth of Actaeon, whom she had changed into a stag to punish him for peeping while she was bathing. There is a painting of 1530 by Cranach depicting Apollo and Diana, in which Diana is sitting naked on a stag. The Catania card fits perfectly into our scheme; it depicts *Temperance* as one of the forms of the Triple Goddess of the moon, who was Diana or Ceres or the Great Mother on Earth. The Catania pack must have followed the standard order, in which *Temperance* is a goddess rather than a Virtue.

The sphere of the moon, the lowest of the planets, was the frontier between Eternity and the worlds of Time. Above the moon all was immutable, aethereal. Below the moon, in the spheres of the four elements, everything was mutable and impermanent, subject to Time and change, growth and decay, birth and death.

It was the chasm between Eternity, above the sphere of the moon, and the worlds of Time, below the moon, that had been symbolized by the cliffs of the Visconti-Sforza pack, the red cliffs which start in *Death*. And it was this chasm that was bridged by *Temperance*, who was herself the Earth Mother but who through her participation in the threefold nature of the goddess of the moon could transcend the boundary between the worlds and could rise above the red cliffs of the sphere of Fire, up to the realms of immortality.

The Mantegna prints, then, reflected a world picture in which the primary powers of generation were symbolized by the sun and the moon in their chariots. The Lord and the Lady of Generation had delegated the exercise of their powers to the three angels of generation. Chief of these was Cosmico, the angel of the sun, whose field was the whole of the cosmos. He in turn passed down his power to Chronico, the angel of the moon who controlled the frontier between Eternity and the sublunar worlds of Time. Last in the chain came Iliaco, the angel who attended to generation in the terrestrial world, through man and woman.

The tarot trumps show us a world picture which is broadly similar. In the Realm of Eternity the powers of generation are carried by *The Sun* and *The Moon*, and are passed down through *Temperance*, who bridges the chasm between Eternity and the worlds of Time. Finally in the chain of generation comes Cupid, *Love*.

Temperance, as one of the forms of the Triple Goddess of the moon, and *Love*, as an angel of the sun, form the links between the three Realms.

The importance of the sun and moon in this structure is clear. We now need to take a rather broader look at the part played by astrology in the medieval world scheme. Once again a set of prints will be very helpful.

Chapter 8

The Children of the Planets

Taking a last look at the field of early Italian engraving, there is one more series which is of great interest to us, the prints usually called the Children of the Planets, depicting the influences of each of the seven planets on human life.

There are quite a number of different sets of prints on this theme, from Northern countries as well as from Italy. Of the Italian engravings the earliest set probably comes from Florence and dates from around 1460-1463. A second set, mostly fairly close copies of those, though often reversed, seems to have been issued around 1464-1465. Reproductions of both sets can be found in Hind. Several others followed during the next hundred years or so.

The woodcut shown in Figure 11, depicting the Children of the Moon, is from a German or Netherlandish set of around 1460 or perhaps a little earlier. This has been chosen for illustration here because the bold manner of the design brings out the chief figures particularly clearly, but the contents are substantially the same in the Italian versions.

Like the Triumphs of Petrarch, the Children of the Planets were amongst the earliest of the secular works of Italian engravers and followed a theme which was already well known and popular in art, so that the engraver could have been fairly sure they would sell well.

That astrology played a great part in the life of Italy in those times has long been recognized. Burckhardt for example, in *The Civilisation of the Renaissance in Italy,* devoted a long section to its influence. It was taught in schools as part of the accepted explanation of how the universe worked. It was taught in universities as part of the study of medicine. It was fundamental in the fifteenth-century world picture. Even though by then people no longer really believed in the planetary gods as deities, they were still widely regarded as valid symbols or allegorical expressions of the different types of power and energy at work in the cosmos; and in that sense the planetary gods were still living forces. Everyone would have been broadly familiar with the symbolism of the planets and the signs of the zodiac.

The theme underlying all astrology is that the cosmos is a single living organism, all the parts of which are connected with each other so that what happens in one part of the universe may be reflected in sympathetic happenings in another. Heaven and Earth are bound to each other by this universal sympathy, and the movements of the planets in the heavens, typifying the various forces and energies of the universe, the macrocosm, will be reflected in the life of man, the little world, the microcosm.

The sun and the moon and the other planets, the wandering stars, were seen to

Figure 11.   The Children of the Moon
            German or Netherlandish woodcut (c.1460)

move against the background of the fixed stars, the constellations of the zodiac. To the ancients the essential characteristic of life was movement, and it was because the planets moved in this way against the background of the stars of the zodiac that they had been believed to have individual lives and energies of their own and came to be regarded as gods who had the power to influence the terrestrial world.

The planets thus represented the different types of power actively at work in the universe. The signs of the zodiac on the other hand were constellations of fixed stars which kept the same unchanging positions relative to each other; they represented eternal but more passive qualities in the universe, qualities which were stable and unvarying. The movements of the signs of the zodiac were the movements of the heavens as a whole, rather than individual movements like those of the planets.

Each of the planets was thought to follow perpetually its own individual pattern of movement, its own cyclical progress through the heavens. But there were sympathies and antipathies, both between the planets themselves and also between the planets and the signs of the zodiac; and the progressions of the planets in their courses into favourable or unfavourable mutual aspects, or into sympathetic or unsympathetic zodiacal signs, would bring about corresponding changes in their affects and in their influences on the world below.

The movements of the planets, themselves immutable in their natures, were thus the cause of mutability on Earth.

Human beings, as well as animals and plants and the rest of the sublunar creation, would respond strongly to the influence of a planet if their own natures were astrologically akin to it. This might be, for example, because that planet had been powerful at the time of birth, perhaps because it had then been rising over the eastern horizon or had been strongly placed in some other way. This would make a person sensitive to its influence for the whole of his life, and because his destiny would be

bound up with its movements he was said to be a 'child' of that planet.

This idea of the 'children' of the planets became extended to cover not only individuals born at particular times but also whole classes and groups of people whose occupations and activities were thought to have affinity with a planet and to be specially influenced by it. It was believed that natural gifts, and thus also position and calling, were associated with certain physical temperaments which were the result of the dominance of qualities of hot or cold, dry or moist, and which were influenced by the planet which transmitted a particular combination of those elemental qualities most strongly.

Taking this a little further, countries and institutions and even material objects were also believed to have their affinities with the planets and were brought into the scheme by analogies.

It was in fact a world picture founded on symbolism and thinking by analogy. By the later Middle Ages astrology had developed into a vast system of 'correspondences', in which virtually everything whether material or spiritual was classified as being of the nature of a planet or of a sign of the zodiac. These astrological correspondences were fundamentally an expression of what were felt to be natural sympathies and harmonies in the universe, with all things in creation being symbols of more profound underlying realities.

The theme of the influences of the planets became a frequent one in medieval art — in sculpture in churches, in elaborate schemes of interior decoration in the great mansions and in public buildings, in paintings and in illuminated manuscripts; and it was this system of astrological correspondences which lay at the back of the prints of the Children of the Planets.

The prints were usually in sets of seven, one print for each of the seven planets known to antiquity, showing the classes of people and the activities and things thought to come under the rulership of that planet.

Thus the moon was considered to be the

ruler of the element of water, and of change and mutability, magic and deception; and so the print for the Children of the Moon would show castles surrounded by wide moats, men swimming or fishing or catching ducks, watermills, a wayward donkey, a magician at his table performing conjuring tricks; and in the heavens Luna would ride in her chariot, through her zodiacal sign of Cancer (Figure 11).

Saturn was the ruler of earth, restriction, wisdom and old age and death; and so his print would show farmers cultivating the earth, prisoners, hermits, old men — and in the background there might be a gallows as a reminder of death. In the heavens Saturn would ride in his chariot, with his scythe, in his signs of Capricorn and Aquarius. Popes would be shown in the prints for Jupiter, and soldiers were Children of Mars.

It has been shown in earlier chapters that the tarot seems originally to have been based on the Triumphs of Petrarch, with the trumps falling into four main groups of five cards each, but that in a reorganization of the pack evidenced by the six new cards in the Visconti-Sforza set the trumps now seem to depict the three worlds, with the cards falling into three main groups of seven. Those new cards of the Visconti-Sforza pack are thought to be Ferrarese and to date from around 1480-1490.

The astrological motif in art was particularly strong at Ferrara. The Mantegna Tarocchi, of around 1465, which almost certainly came from there, show strong astrological elements, overtly in the figures of the seven planetary gods, more subtly in the figures of the angels of generation, ministers of the sun and moon. There are too the famous astrological frescoes of the Palazzo Schifanoia, painted around 1470. Ercole d'Este in particular, who became second duke of Ferrara in 1471, is known to have been deeply interested in astrology; and

his wife too, Eleonora of Aragon, would ask for astrological advice on her problems.

In this setting, it becomes a fairly strong probability that the twenty-one trumps of the Visconti-Sforza pack, in its reorganized form with the six new cards, were now meant to illustrate the workings of the seven planets in the three worlds.

The tarot pack in its new form could in a sense be regarded as a kind of enlarged version of the Children of the Planets, expanded so that the three sets of seven trumps would now illustrate the influences of the seven planets not only in the world of everyday life but also in the Realms of the Soul and of Eternity.

Strict proof that the underlying structure of the tarot pack was now an astrological one is not easy. The difficulty lies in the very nature of all symbolism, that it can usually be interpreted in more than one way; and this is particularly so with astrological symbolism because its scope had become so very wide.

What can be done however is to demonstrate the very close congruence between the trumps and a planetary structure, by the use of a framework based on three sets of the seven planets, representing our three Realms. If it can be shown that the tarot trumps fit into this planetary framework in so orderly and consistent a fashion as would be unlikely by pure chance, we may reasonably conclude that the plan of the tarot pack had now in fact become an astrological one.

Particularly in our first set, our Realm of Man, the prints of the Children of the Planets will provide a relatively objective control and check on the activities to be attributed to the various planets.

Before coming to the form to be taken by our planetary framework it may be useful to give an outline of the natures traditionally ascribed to the seven planets.

Chapter 9

The Planetary Gods

In the early days of Christianity the Church had frowned on astrology, linked as it was with pagan planetary gods who were felt to be its competitors. In the Middle Ages this attitude was gradually relaxed. One of the reasons for this was that by then people had ceased to believe in the planetary gods as deities; by Renaissance times their names were used largely as metaphors for the natural or psychological forces thought to be associated with the various planets. The name Venus for instance would be used for what today we might call the pleasure principle, but it was still generally accepted that this could be stirred up by the actual movements of the planet, even though belief in the planetary deity had faded.

The planets were in fact now regarded as part of God's plan for the cosmos. They were instruments for the carrying out of his Providence; and their rhythmic cycles, the rhythms of Nature from which they were unable to depart, had been fixed by God as part of His law. The seven planets were part of His scheme for the bringing down into manifestation on Earth of the divine influence, through seven veins.

The sun was taken as a symbol of Christ or of the Holy Spirit, its beams shining down on mankind as a gift of divine love and grace, and the moon too was often brought into the plan, with the Virgin Mary taking over some of the attributes of Diana the virgin goddess of the moon. Representations of the planets and the signs of the zodiac became increasingly frequent; astrological symbolism had in fact become accepted into Christian art.

By the fifteenth century, when the tarot was born, the cosmological beliefs of a more or less educated European man or woman were often a rather curious mixture of Christianity and astrology, with God and His angels in Heaven contemplating the cyclical movements of the planets which had been established at the Creation and which would influence conditions down on Earth, while the Devil was lurking to snatch any unfortunate souls whose free will had not been strong enough to resist the temptations stimulated by the planetary movements.

There were of course plenty of formal textbooks of astrology, many of them translations from the Arabic, but in the minds of most people their ideas about the natures of the planetary forces had largely been gathered from the stories about the planetary gods learnt in school from the classical poets, especially Ovid, or from the increasingly frequent use of classical themes in Renaissance art. For the more studious there was a textbook of mythology by Boccaccio, which summarized the doings and natures of the gods.

To understand the world picture of a typical Italian man or woman who might play cards at home or at Court, we have then not only to look at official religion, we have also to take more than a casual glance at the allegorical meanings given to the classical gods in the Renaissance.

Just as the seven planets were now all regarded as part of a single plan laid down by God, so too it was stressed in allegory that the seven planetary gods were all members of a single family. They were all inter-related, even if sometimes a bit scandalously. There were many conflicting stories about the exact details of their parentages, but a popular version of their genealogy might go something like this.

Saturn was the oldest of the planetary gods and had once reigned both in Heaven and on Earth. He was a rather strict and severe god, but under his rule most people had led happy and well ordered lives. However he had an unfortunate habit of eating his own children, his own creations — *tempus edax rerum*, Time, devourer of things.

His son Jupiter eventually rebelled and deposed him, after having first emasculated him so as to put an end to that side of his activities. Saturn, deprived of his virility, then retired into deep thought and contemplation.

Jupiter thus became King of Heaven. His was a much more expansive nature. By Latona he became the father of the twins Apollo the sun and Diana the moon. By Juno he was the father of Mars, by Dione of Venus, and by Maia of Mercury. By his sister Ceres he was the father of Proserpine; and with various other ladies he also fathered a rather large number of minor gods and goddesses. He was the Father of the Gods.

Jupiter proceeded to establish religion, so as to secure a proper degree of reverence for himself as King of Heaven. He also established new laws and new order; but being so much occupied in fatherhood in Heaven he did not have a great deal of time to spare for what was going on down on Earth, so he would send his son Mercury, his messenger, to keep an eye on things down there.

Every now and then Mercury would report back to his father to tell him what was happening on Earth and how his laws were being kept or, more often, broken. When something particularly annoyed him Jupiter might rather grumpily throw down a thunderbolt and kill a few people, and he would then send Mercury to take the souls of the offenders down to his brother Pluto, King of the Underworld, with a request that they be given exemplary punishment there. Occasionally, when he was in a good mood, he would send his blessings to mankind with perhaps an inspirational message or two, and when he was feeling particularly benign he might send another of his sons, Bacchus, with a gift of wine. But on the whole Jupiter was much more concerned with Heaven than with Earth. Taking full charge himself of the matter of generation in Heaven, Jupiter was content to delegate the care of generation on Earth to his twin children Apollo the sun and Diana the moon.

To mankind the business of the continuation of life on Earth was of course quite the most important and pleasurable thing, so that although the required formal reverence was duly paid to Jupiter as King of Heaven, this was often a bit perfunctory and in practice in daily and nightly life on Earth much more respect was given to Apollo and Diana, the Lord and the Lady of Generation.

Although very conscientious in making their regular rounds in their celestial chariots to see that the powers of generation were being kept in proper working order, Apollo the sun and Diana the moon had other things on their minds. Apollo was interested in all the nine Muses, and Diana though patroness of fertility in women and of childbirth was for herself much more interested in hunting and distinctly inclined to be chaste.

This meant that Apollo and Diana really could not spare much time for looking after all the mass of little detail necessary to ensure proper love affairs between men and women, so they in turn delegated this part of their work to their half-brother and half-sister Mars and Venus, who were good at that sort of thing and whose son Cupid could be relied on to help in keeping amorous pots boiling.

It would have been from stories of this kind about the planetary gods, then, remembered quite unseriously from their schooldays, and from the growing use in art of allegorical themes from classical myth, that men and women in Renaissance Italy would have formed their impressions of the powers of the seven planets and of the kinds of activities ruled by each of them.

To understand these we have in effect to try to distil the essences of the characters of the seven planetary gods. The contrasting of pairs of opposites is often the clearest way of illustrating the differences of character between the various members of a family, and this kind of approach seems particularly appropriate here since the tarot trumps themselves often fall into natural pairs, like *The Emperor* and *The Empress,* and *The Pope* and *The Popess.*

So far as their effect on life on Earth was concerned, the archetypal pair among the planets were, in practice, Apollo the sun and Diana the moon. They were the two 'lights', the sun ruling the day and the moon the night. Since the moon had no light of her own but only reflected the light of the sun, the two could be regarded as the two sides of a single soli-lunar entity. They were inseparable twins, astrologically as well as in myth. The Lord and the Lady of Generation, they were symbols of spirit and matter, life force and life form.

While the sun and the moon thus formed the main polarity, the other planets too were thought of as pairs of polar opposites. Mars was paired with Venus, and Jupiter with Mercury. Saturn was regarded as forming polarities both with the sun and with the moon, since these two were twins.

The pairing of force and form, active and passive, first found in the sun and the moon was repeated in Mars and Venus, though expressed here more at the emotional and social, or anti-social, level — in war and peace, aggression and harmony, anger and love, dynamism and attraction.

Mars meant action. He was irascible and impetuous, and did not much care whether this led to strife and discord. He was regarded as the minor Infortune. His virtues were those of Hercules — courage and resolution, strength and fortitude.

Venus was desire. She brought desire in all its forms, desire for pleasure, desire for money and standing, desire for all the good things of life, beauty and harmony and love — though in the arousing of sexual desire she was greatly helped by her son Cupid. Hers was the power of attraction rather than action. Just as Mars was the minor Infortune, Venus was the minor Fortune. In medieval times she was sometimes identified with the goddess Fortuna.

Our next pair, Jupiter and Mercury, formed a polarity more at the level of the soul and the mind. In some ways they were rather more alike and less sharply contrasted than other pairs, because Mercury was regarded as convertible in nature. Of all the planetary gods he alone had the power of changing sex, both in himself and in others. He was also capable of taking on to some extent the character of any other god or goddess with whom he was in contact; thus when acting as his father Jupiter's messenger and minister he would take on some of his father's qualities. In Jupiter and Mercury the pairing of force and form could be expressed in terms of inspiration and its dissemination, religion and its teaching, lawgiving and its enforcement.

Jupiter represented spiritual power of all kinds. His was the power to reward by the gifts of the spirit, and to punish by taking those away. He was often depicted in art with a cornucopia in one hand and a thunderbolt in the other. As King of Heaven and spiritual lord of the sky he could be identified in allegory with Christ the King or Christ in Judgement. Within his giving was the power of the spirit both in Heaven and on Earth — religious inspiration, enthusiasm, ecstasy and all those things which go with the wider vision of life. He was the greater Fortune.

Mercury meant communication. As Jupiter's messenger his duties included the promulgation of his father's laws and edicts, and the interpretation of these to mankind; as his enforcement officer he was the psychopomp who took souls from Earth down to the Underworld when their time had come, and very occasionally, as with Proserpine, he brought them back again. He represented too the things of the mind, reason and logic, and skill and craftsmanship. He was also more than a bit crafty, not above a little cheating or quiet lechery with either sex when the occasion presented itself. He was the classic go-between.

Continuing the series of astrological pairs, Saturn was a polar opposite both of the sun and of the moon; he could sometimes be regarded as a black sun, a sun which had burnt out and lost its light.

The sun and Saturn, as a pair of opposites representing force and form once again, expressed the polarity of life and death, of vitality and old age, spirit and wisdom, eternity and time. The moon and Saturn represented the same polarity expressed in rather more emotional and physical ways — birth and death, physical growth and ageing, malleability and rigidity, change and stability, beginnings and endings.

Saturn thus meant restriction and rigidity and all the things which impose limitations. He was regarded as the greater Infortune, but he brought also the wisdom of experience and restraint, concentration and contemplation, depth of thought and reflection.

The virtuous and well ordered lives of men and women on Earth during the reign of Saturn, before Jupiter with his more expansive nature took over and things began to get rather out of hand, were sometimes imagined as a kind of Golden Age. Thus Saturn, the Old God, might be equated allegorically with God the Father, the God of the Garden of Eden before the Fall of Man, the God of the New Jerusalem and the God of the Golden Age to come again at the end of Time, after the Last Judgement.

This mixing of mythology and astrology with Christian teaching and allegory may appear to us today as strange. In the Renaissance, when people were far more familiar with the legends of classical antiquity and also more sophisticated than we perhaps always realize, it was something that seemed quite natural; the planetary gods were being consciously taken as symbols or metaphors for the various forces at work in the cosmos and in human nature.

In looking at the tarot trumps, it has then to be remembered that the mythological and allegorical associations of the planetary gods may often be more important for understanding the characters ascribed to the planets than the technical descriptions to be found in astrological textbooks. But technical astrology would nevertheless offer a valuable framework, a set of pigeonholes as it were into which all things could be sorted and classified according to their planetary and zodiacal natures and correspondences.

The next chapter will show the form of the astrological framework on which the structure of the tarot trumps seems to have been based.

Chapter 10

The Structure of the Tarot Trumps

The argument of this book has been that the tarot trumps, in the reorganized form shown by the Visconti-Sforza pack with its six new cards, now fall into three sets of seven cards each, representing what I have called the Realms of Man, of the Soul, and of Eternity.

The links between the three Realms were provided by cards which played the parts of angels of generation: *Love,* Cupid, generation at the level of the individual man and woman, and *Temperance,* the Earth Mother, generation at the level of the race or species.

With the wide interest in astrology in fifteenth-century Italy and its frequent use as an underlying theme in art, it seemed not unlikely that the three sets of seven cards were based on the seven planets — a kind of elaborated Children of the Planets. This may be tested by showing that the trumps do in fact fit into a framework of this kind so smoothly as would be unlikely by pure chance.

Choosing the form of the framework is not quite as simple as it sounds because there are several possible kinds of order for the seven planets. Of these there is however one kind of order which seems to fit the order of the trumps outstandingly well. This is based on what are called the Essential Dignities of the planets, which express interrelationships between the planets and the signs of the zodiac. The planets were each regarded as more happily placed in some signs of the

zodiac than in others, and were called dignified when in those signs. Many kinds of planetary dignity were recognized in classical astrology, but here we are concerned with only two sorts, rulerships and exaltations.

Each of the seven planets was held to rule or have special affinity with two of the twelve signs of the zodiac, except that the sun and the moon had rulership over only one sign each.

The zodiac was divided into two semicircles, one of which began with the sign Cancer ruled by the moon and worked back to Aquarius, and the other with Leo ruled by the sun, and working forward to Capricorn. Of the two signs ruled by each of the other five planets, one was in the lunar (Cancer) semicircle, and the other in the solar (Leo) semicircle; and one was masculine and the other feminine. (see Table 2).

The signs of the zodiac were regarded as being of masculine or feminine nature in alternate order, with Aries being masculine, Taurus feminine, Gemini masculine and so on. The masculine side of the character of a planet, its more outwardly dynamic influence, was thought to be brought out particularly strongly when in the masculine sign of its rulership, and its feminine side, more inwardly working, when in its feminine rulership.

Besides these rulerships, there was a further

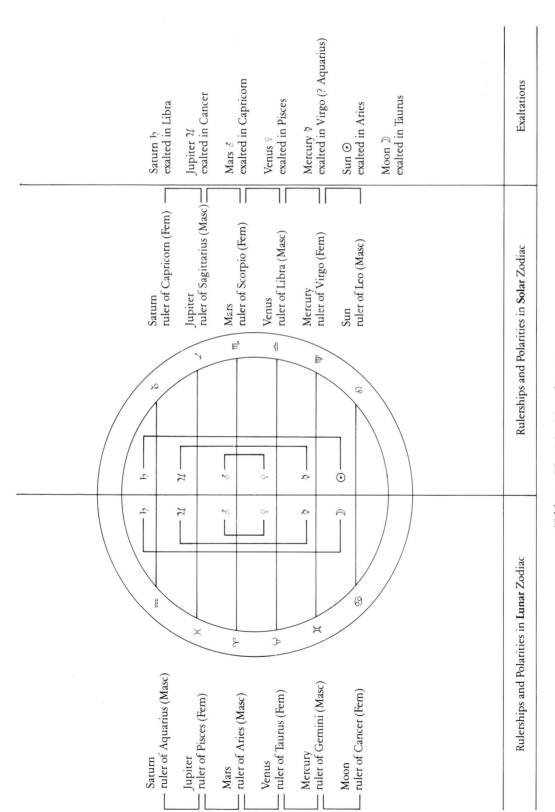

Rulerships and Polarities in **Lunar** Zodiac	Rulerships and Polarities in **Solar** Zodiac	Exaltations
Saturn ruler of Aquarius (Masc)	Saturn ruler of Capricorn (Fem)	Saturn ♄ exalted in Libra
Jupiter ruler of Pisces (Fem)	Jupiter ruler of Sagittarius (Masc)	Jupiter ♃ exalted in Cancer
Mars ruler of Aries (Masc)	Mars ruler of Scorpio (Fem)	Mars ♂ exalted in Capricorn
Venus ruler of Taurus (Fem)	Venus ruler of Libra (Masc)	Venus ♀ exalted in Pisces
Mercury ruler of Gemini (Masc)	Mercury ruler of Virgo (Fem)	Mercury ☿ exalted in Virgo (? Aquarius)
Moon ruler of Cancer (Fem)	Sun ruler of Leo (Masc)	Sun ☉ exalted in Aries
		Moon ☽ exalted in Taurus

Table 2. The Dignities of the Planets.

sign of the zodiac in which the power of a planet was strengthened and in which it could express itself particularly freely. This was called the sign of its exaltation.

A classical myth, well known in medieval times through Macrobius and others, may be brought in here. Souls preparing for birth were said to come down from the heavens into incarnation on Earth through the zodiacal sign Cancer, which was called the Gate of Man. At death the soul would leave the Earth and reascend through the planetary spheres, going out into the Milky Way through the sign of Capricorn, called the Gate of the Gods. The life of man on Earth might thus be regarded, in a sense, as a kind of pilgrim's progress through the signs of the zodiac, from the entrance of the soul into the body at birth in Cancer until its withdrawing from the body at death, in Capricorn.

In the tarot, the first two sets of cards, based on the planets in their rulerships in the lunar and solar halves of the zodiacal circle respectively, could be considered as working in parallel as it were to show the totality of experience in life, through the body (the lunar semicircle) and through the soul (the solar semicircle).

The first set of the planets, ruling the signs of the lunar (Cancer) semicircle of the zodiac, would then symbolize aspects of life in the everyday world in the body, the life of the senses, and would correspond to the cards of our first set of trumps, the Realm of Man. The second set of the planets, ruling the solar (Leo) semicircle, would depict the underlying spiritual circumstances and conditions and would correspond to the cards of our second set of trumps, the Realm of the Soul. The third set of cards, based on the exaltations, would show the nature of the planetary forces and conditions after death, when the soul had withdrawn from the body, our Realm of Eternity. This matches well with the Latin word for exaltations, *altitudines,* heights.

For an astrologically minded designer of a tarot pack, the bringing in of the signs of the zodiac in this way to modify the action of the planets would have offered several advantages.

Firstly and most importantly, it would have allowed him to qualify and distinguish between the influences of a planet in each of the three Realms. To take Mars as an example: in the first set of trumps, the Realm of Man, the nature of Mars as ruler of Aries could be regarded as being expressed by *The Emperor.* In the second set, the Realm of the Soul, the influence of Mars as ruler of Scorpio could be represented by the moral virtue of *Fortitude.* In the third set, the Realm of Eternity, Mars in Capricorn the sign of its exaltation could be allocated to *The Devil,* Pluto, King of the Underworld.

Secondly, the order of the planets stemming from the scheme of zodiacal rulerships (see Table 2) preserves the planetary polarities (Mars — Venus, Jupiter — Mercury, Saturn — sun or moon) discussed in the last chapter. Thus in the Realm of Man, Mars as *The Emperor* would form a polarity with Venus as *The Empress;* Jupiter as *The Pope* would form a polarity with Mercury as *The Popess;* and so on.

Further, since the signs of the zodiac are alternately masculine and feminine, their use to qualify the nature of the planets in this way would also give a polarity between adjacent planets in each of the zodiacal semicircles. Thus Mars in the masculine sign of Aries representing *The Emperor,* material and temporal power, would form a polarity with its neighbour in the zodiacal semicircle, Jupiter in the feminine sign of Pisces, *The Pope,* spiritual and religious power.

The architect of a tarot pack redesigned along these lines would however have had to face a problem: how to reconcile his first two sets of cards representing the seven planets and thus totalling fourteen, with the signs of the zodiac, of which there are only twelve.

In the traditional scheme of planetary rulerships (see Table 2) only one sign each had been given to the sun and the moon, so that in the lunar semicircle there was no sun, and in the solar semicircle there was no moon. So as to bring his first two sets of planetary cards up to seven each, a designer who had used the planetary rulerships of the twelve signs of the zodiac would consequently have had to make two further allocations, a card of solar nature to make up the first set and one of lunar nature for the second set.

It was, I think, to deal with this problem, as well as to provide the links which would join together the three Realms through the chain of being, that in the Visconti-Sforza pack *Love* and *Temperance* were given their special functions as solar and lunar angels of generation.

Love with its distinctive overall red colouring, would fill the place of the missing solar card in the first set. As Cupid, he performed the same duties as the Iliaco of the angels of generation in the Mantegna series, bringing the life-force of the sun down into play on Earth. In the tarot he is often shown as flying down from the sun.

Temperance, who in the Charles VI order had occupied a rather lowly place as a mere Virtue attendant on Laura in her *Chariot,* was now promoted to be a goddess in her own right. As the Earth Mother she bridged the gap between Eternity and the worlds of Time, as Chronico had done in the Mantegna Tarocchi. As one of the three forms of the Triple Goddess of the moon she would fill the place of the missing lunar card of the second set.

From a purely astrological point of view, *Love* and *Temperance,* as soli-lunar figures, might also have been equated with the delightfully named Dragon's Tail and Dragon's Head, the nodes of the moon, often treated in medieval astrology almost as though they were planets.

A framework of three sets of the seven planets can now be constructed along these lines, and the trumps allocated in it. The result is shown in Table 3.

After adding the two links, the solar and lunar angels of generation *Love* and *Temperance,* the first two sets of cards taken in the standard order follow straightforwardly the order of the planets in the two zodiacal semicircles, with only a single exception.

That exception is *The Hermit,* whose special position has already been discussed in

Chapter 6. Because of the difficulty of placing him immediately above God's vicar on Earth, *The Pope,* he had to be given a double role. By allotting him a place in the second set, the Realm of the Soul, he could take over the part of the missing Cardinal Virtue, Prudence. But as a human figure he also belonged in a way to the first set, the Realm of Man; and astrologically too he seems to belong there, as the Saturnian card of the first set.

The third set of cards corresponds to the planets in their signs of exaltation. Here the order is no longer bound by the order of the two zodiacal semi-circles, as it had been in the first two sets. The trumps retain basically the order they had held in the Charles VI type of sequence. The one change is that *The World* is now the final card, instead of *Judgement (The Angel). The World,* the City of God, could then be regarded as symbolizing God the Father, who clearly had to be given top place, and could too be equated with Saturn, the Old God.

Astrologically the three highest cards, representing Heaven and the Holy Trinity, now form a run of the planets exalted in the three cardinal signs of Aries, Cancer and Libra, with the fourth cardinal sign Capricorn falling to *The Devil* as King of the Underworld. *The Sun* (sun in Aries) forms a natural pair with *The Moon* (moon in Taurus).

The soul, after leaving the body in *Death* at the summons of the angel of life and death, *Temperance,* might either ascend straight up to Heaven through *The Moon* and *The Sun,* or might first descend into Hell to *The Devil* (Mars in Capricorn), eventually rising up again after a period in Purgatory through the gateway of *The Tower* (Mercury in Virgo or possibly Aquarius) to the redemption promised by *The Star* (Venus in Pisces).

The individual trumps will be considered more fully in Part 2 of this book, but none of the allocations resulting from our framework seem ill-matched and some of them look strikingly appropriate. *The Magician* for example falls to the moon, as he does in the Children of the Planets (Figure 11). *The Pope* falls to Jupiter, as he does in some sets of the

Children of the Planets, and who is replaced too by Jupiter in certain types of tarot pack. *Justice*, Astraea, falls to Mercury in Virgo (Astraea, goddess of Justice, on leaving the Earth had taken up a place in the zodiac as the sign Virgo). *The Star*, whether taken as the Christian Star of Bethlehem or as Proserpine returning to the upper world with her moisture, looks right as Venus in Pisces.

Altogether, the trumps seem to fit into our planetary framework so well that this could hardly be accidental. An astrological basis for them looks certain.

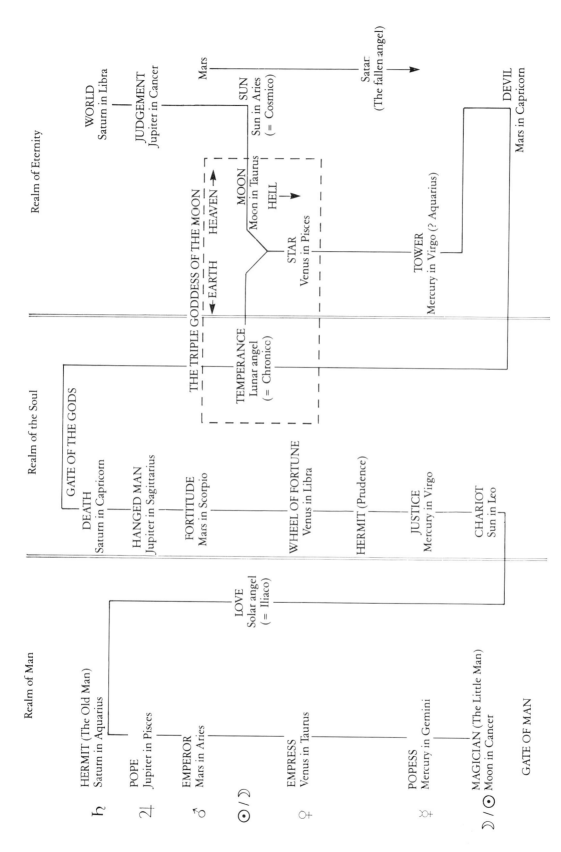

Realm of Man

Realm of the Soul

Realm of Eternity

♄ HERMIT (The Old Man)
Saturn in Aquarius

GATE OF THE GODS

WORLD
Saturn in Libra

DEATH
Saturn in Capricorn

JUDGEMENT
Jupiter in Cancer

♃ POPE
Jupiter in Pisces

HANGED MAN
Jupiter in Sagittarius

Mars

♂ EMPEROR
Mars in Aries

FORTITUDE
Mars in Scorpio

THE TRIPLE GODDESS OF THE MOON

SUN
Sun in Aries
(= Cosmico)

⊙ / ☽

WHEEL OF FORTUNE
Venus in Libra

HEAVEN →

MOON
Moon in Taurus

LOVE
Solar angel
(= Iliaco)

TEMPERANCE
Lunar angel
(= Chronico)

← EARTH

HELL →

STAR
Venus in Pisces

Satar
(The fallen angel)

♀ EMPRESS
Venus in Taurus

HERMIT (Prudence)

☿ POPESS
Mercury in Gemini

JUSTICE
Mercury in Virgo

TOWER
Mercury in Virgo (? Aquarius)

☽ / ⊙ MAGICIAN (The Little Man)
Moon in Cancer

CHARIOT
Sun in Leo

DEVIL
Mars in Capricorn

GATE OF MAN

Table 3. The Structure of the Tarot Trumps.

Chapter 11

Conclusions —
and some guesses

Tarot cards were invented, around 1440, by the adding of a new suit of trumps to the ordinary pack of playing-cards which had been in use in Europe since the 1370s. The earliest known documentary reference to them is from Ferrara, in 1442. Ferrara was a centre of production of finely illuminated manuscripts, and its skilled miniaturists were well equipped for the painting of cards. The tarot may well have been invented there.

The trumps were based originally on the poem cycle of the Triumphs of Petrarch, which around the 1440s became a favourite subject in the decorative arts. As was pointed out by Gertrude Moakley in a paper published in 1956, the trumps were at first called by the same name as the poems — *trionfi* — and they tell the same story. The first and most exhaustive of the literary commentaries on the poem, incidentally, was dedicated to Borso d'Este, ruler of Ferrara from 1441 to 1471.

The type of order followed by the trumps is a useful basis for the classification of the earlier kinds of tarot pack. It has been shown by Michael Dummett that these fall into three main groups. In this book I have called them the Charles VI order (from a pack of around 1470 in the Bibliothèque Nationale), the Steele order (from a list in a fifteenth-century volume of sermons), and the Standard order, the type which eventually became the most widely used, followed in the Marseille style of

pack and many others.

The earliest actually surviving tarot cards are three hand-painted packs probably dating from the 1440s and which may have been painted by Bonifacio Bembo of Cremona. From the many heraldic devices in them it is clear that they were painted for the Visconti-Sforza family, lords of Milan. The early hand-painted cards did not bear numbers in their designs so their proper order may not always be clear, but it is likely that these three 'Bembo' packs originally followed broadly the Charles VI type of order. Based on the Triumphs of Petrarch this was probably the earliest type of sequence, and in it the trumps appear to fall into four main groups of five cards each.

Two of the three 'Bembo' packs are seriously incomplete but the third, called here the Visconti-Sforza pack, is of particular interest because it contains an almost full set of the trumps. It was probably the latest of the three, and made originally around 1446. However it includes six trumps by a later hand, which date from around 1480-1490. These six new cards seem to have been replacements made so as to convert the pack from an earlier form to the new type of order which later became standard.

Instead of the four main sets of five cards each of the Charles VI type of order the trumps now appear to fall into three sets of seven cards each, representing the three worlds which I have called the Realms of Man, of the Soul, and of Eternity. A look at the Tarocchi of Mantegna, a series of fifty engravings dating from the mid-1460s, shows that these too have an implied structure of three worlds. The three angels of the risings of the stars, Cosmico, Chronico and Iliaco, point to a scheme in which the generative powers of the cosmos were symbolized by the sun and the moon, twin aspects of a soli-lunar entity. The structure of the Visconti-Sforza pack, though not exactly the same, nevertheless shows underlying similarities.

Three of the new cards, *The Moon, The Star* and *Temperance,* form a group representing the Triple Goddess of classical antiquity, whose threefold power as Hecate extended to Heaven in which she was the moon, to Hell in which she was Proserpine, the Venus of the Underworld, and to Earth as Ceres or the Earth Mother, the Great Goddess.

Brought together by the rising of *The Star* (Proserpine-Venus, who returns from the Underworld bringing her moisture), *The Sun* and *The Moon* make love in Heaven, the Realm of Eternity. They pass down the powers of generation through *Temperance* (Ceres), who bridges the chasm between Heaven and Earth, the chasm represented by the red cliffs of the sphere of Fire. Fire alone amongst the sublunar elements had the power of rapidly consuming things and transforming them, turning matter into spirit as it were. It was thus a middle term between Heaven and Earth. To have passed through the fire was to have achieved immortality.

Temperance as the Great Goddess represents the perpetual regenerative cycle of Nature. Controlling life and death, but working at the level of the species rather than of the individual, hers is the Realm of the Soul. She in turn passes down her power to the son of Venus, Cupid, *Love,* who brings together individual man and woman, in the Realm of Man. Love, on all the planes and in all its forms, is thus represented as the grand motive power of the universe. The scheme bears all the marks of Renaissance humanism,

with its use of classical myth as a basis for allegory though put forward in a way which also allows a Christian interpretation.

The wide interest in astrology in fifteenth-century Italy is reflected in the series of prints usually called the Children of the Planets, sets of seven engravings showing the influences of the seven planets in the world of everyday life. It comes to seem more than likely that the tarot trumps, falling into the three sets of seven cards in the new standard order, now form a kind of expanded version of the Children of the Planets, showing the influences of the seven planets not only in the world of everyday life but in all three worlds.

The astrological structure of the trumps could be tested against a framework of three sets of the seven planets, looking to see whether the trumps fit neatly into it. A scheme based on the Essential Dignities of the planets in the signs of the zodiac was found to fit particularly well and had the advantage of allowing distinctions to be made between the different effects of a planet in each of the three worlds. The resulting structure was shown in Table 3.

The individual cards will be considered more fully in Part 2 of this book, but after making the single adjustment needed to deal with the dual role given to *The Hermit* all the trumps fit into our framework so smoothly that it looks almost certainly right. The standard sequence of the tarot must in fact have been based on three sets of the seven planets.

Probably the main reason why the planetary nature of the trumps has not been clearly seen lies in the kind of astrology involved, in which the meaning often has to be sought as much in the mythology of the planetary gods and goddesses as in textbook definitions of planetary influences. It takes us into a strange world in which knowledge of the histories of the gods was needed to understand the forces and energies at work in the cosmos and which would influence the life of man.

We end this chapter with some speculations. We have no clear lead to the identity of the person who first devised the tarot, around 1440. Maybe he was an early humanist who thought that the bringing in of Petrarch's poem would lend a proper moral tone to the game of cards, so that it could be played on Sundays — or perhaps he was an artist working on an illuminated manuscript of the Triumphs, who one day suddenly thought that his little pictures would make a fine pack of cards. But whoever the original inventor may have been, the rather distinctive features of the six new cards of the Visconti-Sforza pack suggest that we can make a guess at who it was who around 1480-1490 gave the pack its new form; who it was who worked out the programme for the reorganization of the pack into its new sequence, rather than the artist who actually painted the new cards.

The point has already been made that the six new cards do not show any Visconti-Sforza devices in their designs, suggesting that by then the pack was no longer in the hands of the court of Milan. The new cards are thought to have come from Ferrara. The new card for *Fortitude* depicts Hercules slaying the Nemean lion with his club, the first of his labours. The Hercules motif is known to have been used in the ducal palaces at Ferrara, as an allusion to the reigning Duke Ercole (Hercules) who in his younger days had won a reputation for courage and bravery.

In the new standard order of the pack *Fortitude* was now placed immediately above *The Wheel of Fortune,* in effect showing the constancy and perseverance of Fortitude overcoming the vicissitudes of Fortune. The theme was not uncommon in medieval times — it had been used by Petrarch, for example — but there is evidence that it was regarded as especially appropriate as a tribute to Duke Ercole. In 1501 envoys were sent from Ferrara to Rome to make arrangements for the marriage of Lucrezia Borgia, the daughter of the Pope, to Alfonso, eldest son of Duke Ercole. Gregorovius, in his life of Lucrezia, gives the text of a letter of January 2, 1502, to Duke Ercole, from the Ferrarese ambassadors, describing the festivities held in Rome to honour the envoys and to mark the

forthcoming marriage.

One of the main items chosen for these celebrations was the performance of a ballet in which Hercules with lion's skin and club overcame Fortune and chained her, releasing her only on the condition that she would never do anything against the Houses of Ercole or of Borgia. This is the theme found in the Visconti-Sforza cards. It looks as though the reason for the new Hercules card for *Fortitude* was to pay a compliment to Duke Ercole. It is difficult to see any other reason for its introduction. It did not form part of the red cliff series, to which all the other five new cards belong; nor was it connected with the Triple Goddess, the other main theme introduced then. In the earliest of the three 'Bembo' packs — the Visconti di Modrone set — *Fortitude* had already appeared in the form of the lady subduing the lion which later became the conventionally accepted design and which we may guess was probably also the form of the Visconti-Sforza card before its replacement by the new Hercules version. The new card seems in effect to have been a personal tribute to Duke Ercole, a private heraldic device as it were.

It looks then that the Visconti-Sforza pack had now come into the hands of the court of Ferrara, and we may reasonably look in those circles for our designer. He was probably fairly close to the Duke, being allowed to reorganize a pack regarded as a work of art and able to have the new cards painted by the court miniaturists. The use of the astrological scheme of the Essential Dignities and the rather special emphasis on the sun and the moon suggests a fairly considerable knowledge of astrology. He must also have had the rather special artistic turn of mind which would allow him to indicate how astrological types were to be translated into symbolic paintings. From the classical motifs he was almost certainly of strongly humanistic leanings. Since the figures of the Triple Goddess were dressed in classical style they were likely to date from not earlier than about 1480 — before that date they would more probably have been represented in contemporary

Renaissance dress, rather than classically.

The names of several astrologers at the court of Ferrara in the late fifteenth century are known from the Estense library. In 1912 Aby Warburg was able to identify one of them as having been responsible for drawing up the programme for the astrological frescoes of the Palazzo Schifanoia at Ferrara, painted around 1470. His name was Pellegrino Prisciani.

Prisciani was a remarkably versatile man, as has been shown in an article by A. Rotondò which gathers together much of what is known about him. Born around 1435, the son of a courtier at Ferrara, by 1456 he was already employed at the university. Later he became one of the professors of astronomy there, and his letters show a deep interest in astrology as presenting a world picture which stressed the underlying unity of the whole universe. He had considerable knowledge also of art and architecture, and in 1469-1470 he was one of a group of experts charged with superintending the execution of the Schifanoia frescoes, planned on an astrological basis.

Besides teaching at the university, at various times he acted as archivist, librarian and historian of the court. He had a wide knowledge of classical authors; a letter from Isabella d'Este, daughter of Duke Ercole, to Francesco Gonzaga comments, perhaps with her tongue slightly in her cheek, on the very large number of classical quotations which he brought into his conversation. On several occasions he acted as Ferrarese ambassador at Venice — a rather tricky job — and later at Rome. His letters show that he was on close terms with Duke Ercole and also with his wife Eleonora to both of whom he would from time to time give astrological advice. He gave an oration at the wedding of Alfonso d'Este and Lucrezia Borgia. It has been said of him that he was probably the most learned man in Ferrara of his day.

It is now accepted that the Mantegna Tarocchi almost certainly came from Ferrara, because of very close resemblances of style to the Schifanoia frescoes. Given his position at Ferrara university and his known connection with the drawing up of the programme for the

frescoes, it becomes extremely probable that Prisciani would at least have been aware of the Mantegna prints. Indeed, going a little further, he might very well himself have been responsible for drawing up the programme for them. The use in the prints of the three angels of the risings of the stars appears to be unique, but derived as they are from astronomical theory and depending ultimately on solar symbolism, one may think that they must have been evolved by someone with technical knowledge of astronomy as well as of traditional astrological symbolism. Pellegrino Prisciani was a professor of astronomy. A letter of 1484 quoted by Rotondò shows that he laid overriding importance on the sun in the ordinance of the universe.

At the very least it can be said of him that he would have understood the allegory of the three angels in the Mantegna Tarocchi and would have been able to see how it could be adapted for an astrologically-based set of playing-cards. Moreover he would have known that Prudence had been shown in the Mantegna series with two faces, symbolism befitting the special dual role given to *The Hermit* in the trumps.

There are many unpublished manuscripts by Pellegrino Prisciani in Italian libraries, and it may be that one of these days something will turn up that will confirm or refute his part in all this. For the present we must leave it that he looks a very strong candidate for having given the tarot the form in which we know it today.

Connected to some extent with this is the question of whether there is some kind of secret teaching underlying the structure of the trumps. It is clear that there are several levels of interpretation. At the primary level there is the tarot as a pack of playing-cards, for the game of tarot. Perhaps there may too have been an element of 'Happy Families', with some of the cards depicting members of the ducal courts to which the packs belonged.

The origins of the trumps in the Triumphs of Petrarch make it likely that they also had a secondary purpose, for instruction. The poem had always been recognized as a moral allegory, and the very long commentaries written about it in the Renaissance make it seem almost inevitable that the cards too must have been used at times for moralized exposition. Indeed the Steele sermon itself must remind us that they were used as a text for preaching.

Later in the fifteenth century the trumps were given an astrological structure. Most of the hermetic books of the *Corpus hermeticum* had been translated into Latin by Ficino in Florence in 1463, and had aroused wide interest. They had been printed at Treviso in 1471, at Ferrara in 1472, and later in many other editions. Prisciani with his strong humanist interests and his sun-centred astrology must certainly have studied them. If, as I think, the programmes for the reorganized Visconti-Sforza pack and perhaps

also for the Mantegna Tarocchi were drawn up by him or by someone in his circle at the court of Ferrara, it becomes likely that the plan of the trumps was influenced to some extent by the astral mysticism which had been stimulated by the hermetica. Man the microcosm was to harmonize himself with the macrocosm, the cosmos, through prayer and through meditation on images which, if properly made to their true pattern, would respond to and draw down the beneficent rays and influences of the planets and especially of the sun.

To go further is beyond the scope of this book, but it is a delectable thought that something of the fascination of the tarot may come from the Renaissance cult of magical images.

PART 2

The Symbolism
of the Trumps

Chapter 12

The Trumps Considered

The structure of the tarot trumps in the standard order has been set out in Table 3 showing how they fall into three sets representing the influences of the seven planets in the three worlds which I have called the Realms of Man, of the Soul, and of Eternity.

The first two of these sets represent the planets in their zodiacal rulerships and follow the order of the zodiacal semicircles shown in Table 2, beginning with the moon in Cancer for the first set and with the sun in Leo for the second set. The solar and lunar angels of generation serve as links between the three Realms.

The third set shows the planets in their signs of exaltation. The order here centres on the moon, who in her triple form as Trivia commands the three roads leading to Heaven, to Hell, and to Earth.

For discussion it will be easiest to take the three sets separately. No attempt will be made to give long lists of associations for the cards. It is intended to sketch the outlines of their symbolism only sufficiently to show how they fit into the planetary structure, offering firm ground as a starting point for those who may wish to use them for divination or the development of fantasy, or for meditation. Small illustrations have been included to show how the Marseille pattern is related to the Visconti-Sforza set.

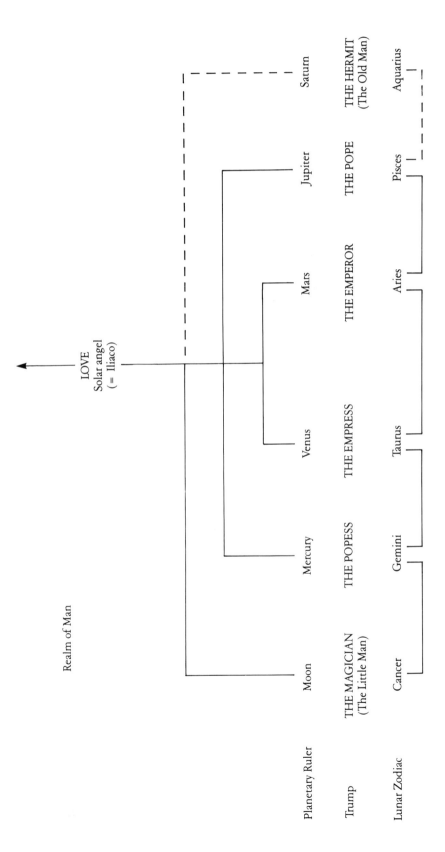

Table 4. The Astrology of the Trumps — First Set.

First Set
Trumps 1 to 6, and 9 (see Table 4)

The planetary framework here follows the lunar half of the zodiacal circle, running from Cancer back to Aquarius. This is lunar consciousness, everyday consciousness, as it were.

This first set of seven trumps depicts the world of human activity, the world of everyday life and personality, the world of here and now which I have called the Realm of Man. The cards here show purely human figures, rather than the allegorical and mythological or theological figures of the later parts of the pack. In a broad way this set corresponds to set E of the Mantegna Tarocchi, the Ranks of Man and the sphere of the element Earth.

The allocation of the cards to the planets runs straightforwardly with the single exception of *The Hermit.* As already discussed *The Hermit* leads a double life. As the Virtue of Prudence he belongs to the second set, the Realm of the Soul, and in the standard order he is rightly placed there, as number 9 in the sequence. There he has retired to his hermitage, and has withdrawn from the social order. But he has not yet quite shuffled off his human existence. His body still has a hold on his soul, even if only a tenuous one, through memory; and in that sense he still has a part to play in the first set, the Realm of Man. Astrologically too he still belongs here, as the first Saturnian card.

The prints of the Children of the Planets are particularly useful in connection with the first set, providing a relatively objective check on the kinds of occupations and activities which were regarded in the fifteenth century as coming under the influences of each of the seven planets. Hermits for example are always shown as children of Saturn.

The planetary scheme provides an explanation of some otherwise rather puzzling things. It has long been recognized that *The Pope* and *The Popess* sometimes gave offence to religious sentiment; as far back as the fifteenth century the writer of the Steele sermon had been complaining of these two cards. From time to time efforts were made to replace them. In some packs *The Pope* was changed to a *Jupiter* (see Figure 12c), which fits in correctly with our astrological framework; *The Popess* then had to become *Juno,* the sister and wife who plagued him (see Figure 12d).

In the so-called Belgian pattern *The Pope* has become a *Bacchus* (see Figure 12e), perhaps a rather literal interpretation of the medieval Latin tag *bibere papaliter,* to drink like a pope. In this type of pack *The Popess* is supplanted by *The Spanish Captain* (see Figure 12f), who at first sight has nothing at all in common with her. But once it is accepted that *The Popess* takes her place in the first set of trumps as a child of Mercury (astrologically a sexually ambiguous and ambivalent planet), then her replacement by another Mercurial card is no longer surprising. *The Spanish Captain* is a Mercurial character of the first order — and also, like Pope Joan, a bit of an imposter.

Following this up a little further suggests an explanation for another type of early trump, sometimes called *The Falconer* from his having a bird on his wrist (see Figure 12g, h, i). Lemprière says that Mercury could be represented with a cock on his wrist, as a symbol of vigilance. He might carry a purse, because he was the god of merchants. He had a short sword. These may appear in *Falconer* cards.

One of the *Falconer* cards (see Figure 12h) also shows the toothed escapement wheel of a clock. Clocks, or clock parts, were often shown in prints of the children of Mercury as symbols of the ingenuity and inventiveness which he bestowed. Confirmation of the escapement wheel as a symbol of Mercury is to be found in a photograph of one of the so-called Rosenthal cards, *The Sun* (see Figure 12j). Under the image of the sun are shown the toothed escapement wheel (Mercury) and a fleur-de-lys (Venus). The point here is that in classical astrology Mercury and Venus were called the Companions of the Sun, because to an observer on Earth they could never be very far distant from the sun.

The authenticity of some of these cards has been questioned and it may be that some of them are copies of originals that have now disappeared, but this is not really material in the present context, where we are concerned with the symbolism of the cards rather than with their age.

It seems then that *The Falconer* was intended to represent a child of Mercury and was a predecessor of *The Spanish Captain*. Both were substitutes for *The Popess,* also a Mercurial card. Though not in itself important, the point adds further support to the planetary structure of the tarot.

(a)   (b)   (c)   (d)

(e)   (f)   (g)   (h)

(i)   (j)

Figure 12.   THE POPE and THE POPESS, and their variants.
(a) and (b) The Pope and The Popess in the Marseille pattern (18c.); (c) and (d) their
substitutes, Jupiter and Juno, in the Besançon pattern (18c.); (e) and (f) other substitutes,
Bacchus and The Spanish Captain, in the Belgian pattern (18c.); (g), (h), (i) Falconer
cards, apparently predecessors of The Spanish Captain as substitutes for The Popess; (g)
may be a later imitation of some lost original (Dummett, p.73); (h) is from the
'Goldschmidt' pack (15c. — Kaplan, p.110); (i) is from a photograph of the 'Rosenthal'
cards, present whereabouts unknown (Kaplan, p.99); (j) The Sun, from the same
photograph as (i) (Kaplan, p.99). It shows a toothed escapement wheel like that in (h);
a symbol of Mercury (see p.81-2).

—83—

1. The Magician
(The Little Man)
Moon in Cancer

Visconti-Sforza

Marseille

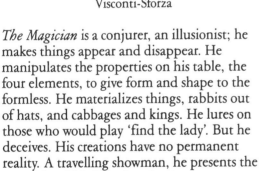

The Magician is a conjurer, an illusionist; he makes things appear and disappear. He manipulates the properties on his table, the four elements, to give form and shape to the formless. He materializes things, rabbits out of hats, and cabbages and kings. He lures on those who would play 'find the lady'. But he deceives. His creations have no permanent reality. A travelling showman, he presents the spectacle of life. The show begins.

The moon was traditionally associated with magic and the control of the forces of nature. Like *The Magician,* the moon caused things to appear and disappear, in the rhythms and cycles of nature and in the changing light of her monthly cycle. She symbolized change,

transition from one state of being to another, birth; the channelling into physical form of all the celestial powers of the universe.

In classical myth the sign Cancer, ruled by the moon, was the Gate of Man, through which souls had to pass when coming down into incarnation on Earth. Cancer, cardinal and watery, was the waiting room for birth, the womb of the cosmos.

The prints of the Children of the Moon confirm the allocation of *The Magician* to the moon, showing him standing behind a table which carries his equipment (see Figure 11).

The Magician is a card of change and transformation and fecundity and dreams.

2. The Popess
Mercury in Gemini

Visconti-Sforza

Marseille

The Popess holds a book; she teaches. As her name implies, she is the consort of *The Pope;* her task is to understand his message and to teach it and spread it. She is robed like a nun. Her sexuality is muted or perhaps, like Pope Joan, cryptic.

Mercury was the planetary god of learning and communication and of applied skills and crafts. He was the messenger of Jupiter, the heavenly father and celestial lawmaker. Both sexually and in a more general sense Mercury was inclined to be ambivalent.

The sign Gemini, mutable and airy, would add flexibility and versatility. It was traditionally classed as a double-bodied sign, further emphasizing the ambivalence of Mercury, his ability to absorb from some and give out to others.

The Children of the Planets show teaching as one of the many occupations presided over by Mercury.

In modern packs *The Popess* is often given lunar attributes, and *The Magician* is then treated as a child of Mercury. This transposition is a purely nineteenth century innovation with no roots in tradition; it obscures the underlying symbolism, which is based on a contrast between *The Magician,* dealing with the materialization ruled by the moon, and *The Popess,* more concerned with the things of the mind.

The Popess is a card of teaching and learning, a link between Pope and populace.

3. The Empress
Venus in Taurus

Visconti-Sforza

Marseille

The Empress bears the heraldic devices of *The Emperor;* she is his consort, his desire. She is desire in all its forms, sexual desire, desire for pleasure, desire for beauty and harmony, desire for the good things of this world. She is the pleasure principle. In contrast to *The Popess* she is openly attractive, sexually and sensually. She rules the emotional side of life, rather than the mind.

Venus was the goddess of desire, bestowing the power of attraction and the graces. The sign Taurus, fixed and earthy, adds stability

and also brings out the more practical side of her nature, the desire for marriage and motherhood and social standing, as well as for material possessions and comforts and diamond rings.

The Children of the Planets show Venus presiding over pleasure in all the usual forms, wining and dining, singing and dancing and making love.

The Empress is desire, achieved through attraction.

4. The Emperor
Mars in Aries

Visconti-Sforza

Marseille

The Emperor depicts the Holy Roman Emperor. He holds the orb and sceptre, symbols of temporal power, power in this world. He gets what he wants through action, through force and energy, military strength and temporal power, in contrast to *The Empress,* who gains her desires through her power of attraction.

Mars was the god of force and action, strife and war. The sign Aries, cardinal and fiery, would emphasize the outgoing and extraverted side of his character, the impulsive energy which he would pour into all his activities, his self-assertiveness.

The Children of the Planets show Mars in action and in conflict, as a raider and invader. There is courage and drive and initiative but there is also aggression and rape and pillage and all the forms of force and violence.

The Emperor is temporal power, achieved through action.

5. The Pope
Jupiter in Pisces

Visconti-Sforza   Marseille

The Pope wears the tiara, the triple crown, symbol of power and authority in the three worlds, but his is the spiritual power, the power and authority drawn from Heaven in contrast to the temporal and military power of *The Emperor.* He is the Holy Father, the Vicar of God, and head of the Church on Earth. In one sense *The Popess* could be regarded as the body of the Church through which the message of *The Pope* is to be given out.

Jupiter was the king of Heaven and as celestial ruler and lawmaker he was the god most concerned with religion and with giving inspiration and the wider outlook on life to mankind. The sign Pisces, mutable and watery, would add sympathy and compassion, stressing the unison between the individual

and the universe. The fish was often used as a Christian symbol. Peter the first Pope had been a fisherman, and the ring placed on the finger of a new Pope is called the Fisherman's Ring.

In some sets of the Children of the Planets the print for Jupiter shows a Pope carrying out the coronation of an Emperor kneeling before him. Other sets show the great Italian literary trio, the 'three crowns', Dante, Petrarch, Boccaccio, symbolizing essentially the same idea, the drawing down of inspiration from the heavens and the giving of expression to it in this world.

The Pope is spiritual power, power by inspiration from above.

The Hermit
(The Old Man)
Saturn in Aquarius

Charles VI

Rosenwald (Charles VI order)

The Hermit is the only instance where the standard order of the trumps differs from the order of the planets in the two zodiacal semicircles which form the basic framework of our first two sets.

The Hermit is clearly the first card of Saturnian nature. In all the sets of the Children of the Planets, hermits are invariably shown as children of Saturn. The sign of Aquarius too, fixed and airy, the sign ruled by Saturn in the lunar semicircle of our first set, fits *The Hermit* very well, stressing the independence of his ways of life and thought.

From the purely astrological standpoint it might be expected that *The Hermit* would be found at this place in the sequence, as the Saturnian card which should follow immediately after the Jupiterian card, *The Pope,* in the first set. But the difficulty of this has been seen. As the Vicar of God *The Pope* had to be regarded as holding the top job in the Realm of Man, as he does in the Mantegna series (print E 10), and it would be impossible to treat *The Hermit* as his immediate superior.

The solution adopted was to regard *The Hermit* as having partly withdrawn from our first set, the world of flesh and blood. By

allowing him to enter a hermitage, a retreat amongst the trumps of the second set, the Realm of the Soul, there would no longer be the problem of social precedence; and as Prudence he could there keep company with the other Cardinal Virtues.

Prudence could be shown with two faces, that of an old man looking back to the past and also that of a young girl looking forward to the future. Nevertheless so far as the astrological symbolism is concerned *The Hermit* is best understood as belonging to the first set. There, as the Saturnian card symbolizing contemplative religion, inner faith, he would form a contrasting pair with the outer and mundane religious authority of *The Pope,* Jupiter.

The Hermit, as a child of Saturn, also forms a polarity with *The Magician* (moon). The two might in a way be regarded as contrasting aspects of Merlin, who could be both the Wise Old Man giving sage advice and also the Little Man, the young Magician up to all the tricks of his trade.

There is no suggestion that the order of the trumps needs any kind of rectification. Like Prudence in the Mantegna print, *The Hermit* simply has two guises. He is both the Wise Old Man and also the Cardinal Virtue, Prudence. In one aspect he belongs to the first set, the Realm of Man, in the other to the second set, the Realm of the Soul. Because of the problem of his position in the social hierarchy, the designer placed the card in the second set rather than in the first.

6. Love
(Iliaco)
The angel of the sun

Visconti-Sforza

Marseille

Love appears as Cupid, his bow and arrow pointed down at the lovers. Often he is shown as a winged angel flying down from the sun; it was through love that the life-force of the sun, the generative power of the cosmos, was brought down to mankind from the heavens. Sometimes he is blindfolded, to show the impersonality of the life-force.

Love, with its very human figures of the lovers, is the last card of the first set, the Realm of Man. It is the key card of the set, and in some ways of the whole series. In the Visconti-Sforza pack it has been given a special red colouring, to distinguish it from the rest of the trumps. The red is a background, to symbolize the sphere of Fire through which love comes down to mankind and through which the lovers will pass upward, to Heaven and immortality.

Love was the power through which God ordered the universe, controlling and bringing together and harmonizing all the separate forces. Love brought order to the four elements, saving them from the chaos into which they would have fallen through their conflicting and opposing natures. Love was the driving power of the cosmos.

In the Mantegna series Iliaco, the angel of

heliacal rising, is shown holding the globe of the conjoined sun and moon, symbolizing the generative power of the cosmos being brought down to the human level (see Figure 10). In a heliacal rising, in the dawn light, night and day meet and join briefly together. But each day the sun moves a little further along the zodiac, and stars which could not previously be seen because of the nearness of the sun now become visible in the night sky, the province of the moon; the sun by his movement in his chariot has, as it were, caused the birth of new stars.

The allegory is repeated in the tarot. It is by the moving of *The Chariot,* the solar card which begins the second set, that the cards of the first set are brought to birth in the sublunar world, *The Empress* and *The Emperor, The Popess* and *The Pope, The Magician* and *The Hermit.* And it is *Love,* Cupid the son of Venus, who brings down the power of the sun, to bring them together and create new bodies, new visions of life. As the messenger of the sun he is their moderator, their controller. He is the link from the second set down to the first; he is also the way up from the first set to the second.

This is the card of love in all its forms.

Second Set
Trumps 7 to 14 (see Table 5)

The second set of trumps shows the Realm of the Soul, the world of life and death and of the virtues and moralities. The first set had comprised human figures. The second set consists of allegorical personifications, allegories of the working of the spirit in man; it could be regarded as a kind of Jacob's Ladder, with the angelic Virtues ascending and descending between Heaven and Earth.

The planetary framework here follows the solar half of the zodiacal circle, from Leo forward to Capricorn. This is solar consciousness, soul consciousness, contrasted with the lunar everyday consciousness of the first set. The two sets work in parallel, as the soul with the body.

Just as *Love* was the key card of the first set, so the key card of the second set is *Temperance,* love as the life-force here finding expression in the perpetual cycle of life and death, manifesting first in one vessel, one body, then in another, and another. The positive phase of the life cycle is shown in *The Chariot,* the soul entering into the body to give it life and movement. The negative phase is *Death,* the withdrawing of the soul from the body. The two phases are subsumed in *Temperance;* the whole cycle of life and death belongs to her.

In a broad way the cards of the second set may be compared with set B of the Mantegna Tarocchi, the Virtues and the Angels of Generation, the sphere of the element Fire.

Number symbolism had long been used in the Middle Ages as a way of considering and classifying abstract qualities. I do not think that the trumps as a whole had a numerological basis, but it may have influenced the numbering of some of the cards in the standard order, especially in the second set dealing as this does with abstractions like the Virtues; in particular it may have influenced the positioning of *The Hermit.* A few notes on number symbolism, drawn from Cornelius Agrippa's *Occult Philosophy* (early 1500s, translated into English 1651) have consequently been included here.

Realm of the Soul

TEMPERANCE
Lunar angel
(= Chronico)

LOVE
Solar angel
(= Iliaco)

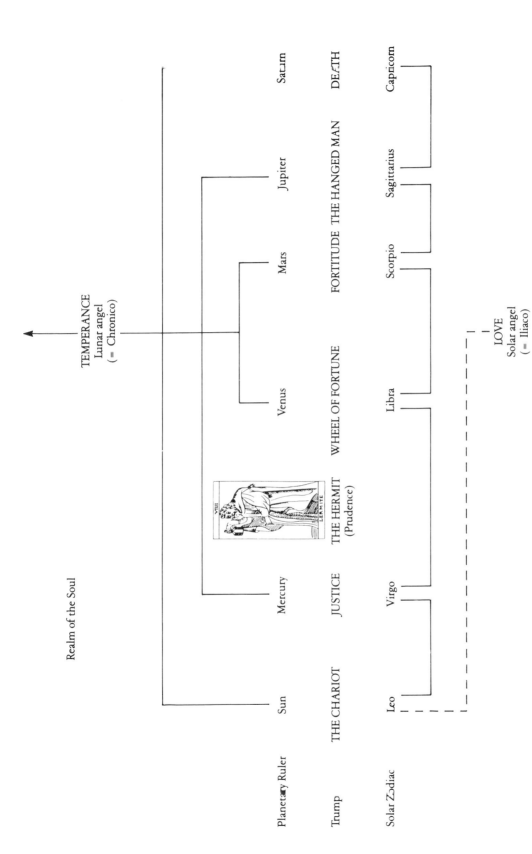

Planetary Ruler	Sun	Mercury		Venus	Mars	Jupiter	Saturn
Trump	THE CHARIOT	JUSTICE	THE HERMIT (Prudence)	WHEEL OF FORTUNE	FORTITUDE	THE HANGED MAN	DEATH
Solar Zodiac	Leo	Virgo		Libra	Scorpio	Sagittarius	Capricorn

Table 5. The Astrology of the Trumps — Second Set.

7. The Chariot
Sun in Leo

Visconti-Sforza

Marseille

The Chariot shows a triumphal car drawn by two horses. Often the occupant is a crowned figure. The Visconti-Sforza card, and also Minchiate designs, depict the occupant as a woman; originally this had been Laura herself celebrating the Triumph of Chastity, but perhaps that idea was not very popular and a change to a male occupant of the car seems to have been made at a fairly early date and soon became the usual form.

The card presents the celebration of a triumph. It symbolizes the spirit of life, the soul entering into the body, to animate it and give it the power of movement, vivifying it; some Minchiate versions carry the legend *Viva viva,* to signify just that. Perhaps it also reflects Plato's simile of man as a charioteer driving two horses, the one spiritual, the other sensual. The writer of the Steele sermon has added a note that the card is the *parvus mundus,* the little world, the microcosm, man.

The spirit of life, vitality, was always associated in astrology with the sun, often depicted as driving his chariot across the sky. The sign Leo, fixed and fiery, would stress the power of the creative life-force entering into the body.

The last card of the previous set, *Love,* had shown Cupid the angel despatched by the sun, the charioteer, to stir up the physical processes of generation and see to the provision of a physical body. *The Chariot,* the first card of the second set, the Realm of the Soul, shows the spiritual side of the process, the joining of the soul to the body to give it life and movement, to give expression to the spirit.

Cornelius Agrippa says of the number seven that:

> the Pythagorians call it the Vehiculum of mans life . . . it contains body, and soul, for the body consists of four elements . . . the number three respects the soul . . . The number seaven therefore, because it consists of three, and four, joyns the soul to the body, and the virtue of this number relates to the generation of men, and it causeth man to be received, formed, brought forth, nourished, live, and indeed altogether to subsist.

This is a card of the spirit of life, vitality.

8. Justice
Mercury in Virgo

Visconti-Sforza

Marseille

Justice shows Astraea, goddess of justice, the lady with the sword and the scales who also stands on top of the Old Bailey, the Central Criminal Court in London. In the Golden Age Astraea had lived on Earth but, shocked and disgusted by the wickedness and impiety which came over mankind, she retired to the heavens where she took up a vacant position in the zodiac and became the sign Virgo. She was the last of the gods and goddesses to leave the Earth, and the myth told that the eventual return of the Golden Age would be marked by her coming back.

Justice was one of the four Cardinal Virtues of antiquity, the others being Prudence, Fortitude and Temperance. She had to do with law in all its forms, the laws of humanity as well as divine law, the laws of Nature as well as of the spirit. She represented the knowledge and administration of law, its application rather than its making which was the province of Jupiter the celestial lawgiver. She was concerned with right conduct, right behaviour towards others and living in concord and friendship with them, and with piety and the observance of religion.

The card *Justice* can be allocated to

Mercury, the son and messenger of Jupiter. The mutable and earthy sign Virgo, besides its connection in myth with Astraea, goddess of justice, would stress the qualities of fine discrimination, critical judgement.

Ficino, in a letter of 1481 quoted by E. H. Gombrich (*Symbolic Images,* p.57) wrote of '. . . Mercurius Jovius, that is Mercury aided by the aspect or some other favour of Jupiter. For it is Mercury who, with that certain vital and prompt liveliness of his, exhorts us always to research into the truth of matters'.

The card reflects the search for truth in all its forms. In the Realm of the Soul it represents those powers of Mercury as the servant of Jupiter which, in the Realm of Man, had been given practical expression in the teaching of *The Popess,* also under Mercury. *The Chariot* had represented the life spirit, the vivifying power in the soul; *Justice* represents the laws and the order through which the life spirit is given play.

In the Middle Ages the concept of the Sun of Justice, *sol justitiae,* had become identified with Christ in Judgement. It may have been partly because of this, as well as because of the hint of the return of Astraea and the Golden

Age, that in the Steele order the card was moved up to become the penultimate card in the pack, above *Judgement (The Angel)* and immediately below the final card, *The World,* the City of God.

Cornelius Agrippa says:

> The Pythagorians call eight the number of justice, and fulness: first, because it is first of all divided into numbers equally even, viz, into four and that division is by the same reason made into twice two, viz, by twice two twice; and by reason of this equality of division, it took to itself the name of justice . . .

This is a card of the search for truth, in righteous conduct as well as in knowledge.

9. The Hermit
(Prudence)
Saturn in Aquarius

Visconti-Sforza

Marseille

The Hermit makes his appearance at this place, in the standard order. His astrological correspondences have already been discussed in the first set, and as the Wise Old Man he belongs there for our planetary framework; but for hierarchical reasons it was not possible to give him the position immediately above *The Pope.*

The difficulty was overcome by allowing him a place in a second set, the Realm of the Soul, where he could be regarded as having withdrawn from the Realm of Man or at least as only barely belonging to it in his retreat, his hermitage. Here he could fill a gap by also playing the part of the missing Cardinal Virtue, Prudence, traditionally a figure of double nature.

In the Charles VI type of order the role of Prudence had been filled by *The World,* with the lady wearing the polygonal halo of the Virtues and standing on the cosmic globe as Miss World (see Figure 2).

For the new standard order of the trumps it was necessary to alter the positions of the Virtues so that they could all be fitted into the second set of seven cards, the Realm of the Soul. This meant having to find another card

instead of *The World* to double for the part of Prudence; and *The Hermit* as a Saturnian was excellently qualified for the job. The association between Prudence and Saturn was a well-established one, explicit in many astrological texts.

Originally the card had probably been Faith. In the Visconti di Modrone pack this had been depicted as a woman holding a cross, but the change to the figure of *The Hermit* must have been made at a very early date as he already appears as such in the Visconti-Sforza cards of around 1446. (In some Minchiate packs, incidentally, *Faith* appears as a bearded monk.)

At first, *The Hermit* was shown holding an hour-glass, marking his connection with the Triumph of Death, the sands of life running out. In the sixteenth century the hour-glass usually became a lantern, probably because in the new standard order he was no longer so closely connected with death but had now taken over the role of Prudence. In one well-known medieval text Prudence had been called the Lantern.

Cornelius Agrippa says that nine was an angelic number because there were nine orders of angels (of which the Virtues were one). Nine was also associated with the Grand Climacteric, nine times seven years, the entry into real old age.

The Hermit is a card both of the contemplative faith of the Wise Old Man looking back on life and of the circumspection and self-knowledge of that very cautious lady, Prudence, looking forward to her reward in Eternity.

10. The Wheel of Fortune
Venus in Libra

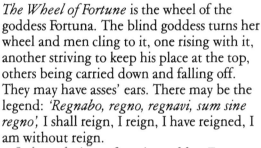

Visconti-Sforza

Marseille

The Wheel of Fortune is the wheel of the goddess Fortuna. The blind goddess turns her wheel and men cling to it, one rising with it, another striving to keep his place at the top, others being carried down and falling off. They may have asses' ears. There may be the legend: *'Regnabo, regno, regnavi, sum sine regno',* I shall reign, I reign, I have reigned, I am without reign.

In later designs often the goddess Fortuna herself is not shown; her wheel is driven round by the apes who climb on it and cling to it in their ambition to be at the top.

The card represents desire and envy and avarice as motivating forces. The symbol of the wheel was a familiar one which had come to be associated particularly with *The Consolation of Philosophy* of Boethius, in the Middle Ages perhaps the most famous of all secular books: true happiness and inner peace and freedom from the anxieties inseparable from changeable Fortune can be found only in the love of wisdom and the love of God.

Probably the original form of the card was Charity; as *caritas* this was the theological Virtue of love towards God and towards our fellow men. In the Visconti di Modrone card

(Kaplan, p.91., Dummett, plate 10) the lady personifying the Virtue of Charity is shown triumphing over the corresponding Vice, a recumbent figure with a prominently uplifted gold finger who is clearly Midas; all that he touched turned to gold, including his dinner. He symbolized avarice, greed, desire for power and money. It is not too difficult to see how he could be transmuted in later packs into the figure of *The Wheel,* which too is often presented as symbolizing greed. In effect the Virtue to be attained is now illustrated by the Vice to be conquered.

Attribution of *The Wheel* to the planet Venus looks right. In medieval times Venus was often not clearly distinguished from Fortuna and like her may sometimes be shown turning a wheel. Traditionally the Lesser Fortune of astrology, Venus was regarded as having something of a double nature, beneficent and harmonious when well placed but easily influenced by other planets and rather apt to turn malign when in low company. The sign Libra, cardinal and airy, would stress this two-sidedness, the symbol of the scales showing the quest for balance and harmony but easily swayed and unbalanced by passing whims and circumstances.

In the Realm of the Soul *The Wheel* represents the emotional forces of desire which in the Realm of Man had found more tangible expression in *The Empress,* also under Venus. It may be contrasted with *Justice* which was more concerned with intellectual knowledge of right behaviour towards others. The inconstancy of Fortune may be contrasted too with the constancy bestowed by the next card, *Fortitude.*

After *The Wheel* in the standard order we reach a turning point. Up to here the trumps are concerned with activities in the world of the living. After this they are oriented more towards death and the life after the soul has left the body, the life of the Realm of Eternity.

The number ten was regarded as completing a cycle. Cornelius Agrippa says that it 'is called every number, or an universall number, compleat, signifying the full course of life'.

The Wheel symbolizes desire, both material and spiritual, as the driving force behind the round of human life, and which needs to be ruled by love.

11. Fortitude
Mars in Scorpio

Visconti-Sforza

Marseille

Fortitude is another of the Cardinal Virtues. The card usually shows a lady either clasping a broken column (a reference to Samson) as in the Charles VI and Minchiate types, or forcing open the jaws of a lion, as in the Visconti di Modrone set and in the Marseille type. Exceptionally, the trump in the Visconti-Sforza pack (one of the six new cards there) shows Hercules with his club, slaying the Nemean lion, the first of his labours (see Figure 1). He is depicted with a scarf patterned with the triple golden rays of the sun to show that there was something of divinity in him; though as he was a mortal, still on this side of *Death,* he was not granted the red foreground reserved for immortals.

The Visconti-Sforza pack seems originally to have been painted around 1446 for the court of Milan. The new cards in this pack are considered to have been painted in Ferrara, probably around 1480-1490, and we may think that by then the pack had somehow found its way to the court there. It seems likely that the new version of *Fortitude* was intended as a tribute to Ercole (= Hercules) d'Este, Duke of Ferrara from 1471 to 1505, who in his younger days had acquired a reputation for courage and bravery. It is known that the Hercules motif was in fact used in this way in the Este palaces of the period, and it is hard to see any other sufficient reason for the making of the new Hercules card. It did not form part of the red cliff series to which all the other new cards belong; nor was it closely connected with the Triple Goddess, the other main theme introduced by the new cards.

The position given in the standard order to *Fortitude,* which now comes immediately after *The Wheel of Fortune,* shows the struggle of Virtue against the allurements and ficklenesses of the goddess Fortuna. This theme was not uncommon in medieval art; indeed in one form it was presented as Hercules at the crossroads between Virtue and Vice. But *Fortitude* could be quite adequately personified as a woman forcing open the jaws of a lion, which became the traditional form in the tarot, and in which shape she had already appeared in the Visconti di Modrone pack. One must think that the main reason for making the change in the Visconti Sforza pack to the new Hercules card must have been as a compliment to the reigning Duke of Ferrara.

Fortitude represents courage in the widest sense, spiritual and moral strength as well as physical, and steadfastness and perseverance.

The card can be allocated to Mars. The sign of Scorpio, fixed and watery, would add emotional intensity and depth to the qualities of bravery and courage. It represents the powers of the soul which, in the Realm of Man, had found expression in *The Emperor,* allocated to Mars in Aries.

Cornelius Agrippa says that, 'the number eleven as it exceeds the number ten, which is the number of the commandements, so it falls short of the number twelve which is of grace and perfection, therefore it is called the number of sins, and the penitent.' The underlying idea again seems to be of the struggle of Virtue against Vice, and of preparation for the next number, twelve, a number of perfection.

Fortitude is a card of courage and boldness, and steadfastness in the face of tribulation and temptation.

12. The Hanged Man
Jupiter in Sagittarius

Visconti-Sforza

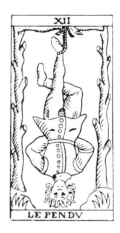

Marseille

The Hanged Man was also called The Traitor. In Florence it was the custom for pictures of traitors to be painted on one of the public buildings. If they had been caught and hanged they were depicted as hanged by the neck, but if they had escaped and were still at large they were to be shown as hanged by the heel. Botticelli once had to carry out paintings of this kind on the orders of the city fathers, after the Pazzi conspiracy of 1478. The Hanged Man was an image that would have been familiar to everyone.

In the tarot the essence of the symbolism is change of allegiance, reversal of point of view, and preparation for death. Coming in the second half of the trumps, after the turning point when the worldly ambitions and desires shown by *The Wheel* were to be conquered by *Fortitude*, *The Hanged Man* shows man suspended between Heaven and Earth, his feet no longer on the ground but now held firmly from above. His attitude to life has changed, his point of view is reversed. He is the man called by his destiny to put forward new teachings. By worldly standards he may seem a traitor, a rebel, a disturber of the state, but he is no longer concerned with mundane

values, in his search for God he is moved only by spiritual ones. After the steadfastness of *Fortitude* he is the soul now ready to take more active steps in spreading the message of the spirit even though this may lead to self-sacrifice and death. St Peter, the first Pope, was said to have been crucified head downwards.

Probably the earliest form of the card was Hope, as in the Visconti di Modrone pack (Kaplan, p.91., Dummett, plate 10) where it shows a woman kneeling in prayer over the figure of Judas, the archetypal traitor, who had hanged himself. In the foreground is an anchor, because 'hope we have as an anchor of the soul, both sure and stedfast, and which entereth into that within the veil' (*Hebrews*, vi, 19). The anchor was thus used as a symbol of the transcendent.

The Hanged Man can be allocated to Jupiter, King of Heaven and god of religion and philosophy. In the first set, the Realm of Man, *The Pope* had been the channel for the influence of Jupiter expressed through the feminine sign Pisces. In this second set *The Hanged Man* shows the influence of Jupiter now acting through the masculine or positive sign of Sagittarius, mutable and fiery, representing a more direct expression of divine spirit. Here Jupiter has imposed a sacrifice on man, inspiring him with higher ideals but not yet setting him entirely free from the body. That he is shown as hanged by the heel rather than by the neck means that he is still in the world of the living.

Justice (Mercury in Virgo) had represented the search for truth. *The Hanged Man* (Jupiter in Sagittarius) shows the sacrifice imposed in that search, the stress and conflict between body and soul.

The sign Sagittarius, the Archer, emphasizes this duality between body and soul. The Archer was often shown as a centaur, half man, half beast. His arrow was said to show the impalement of the body by the arrow of the spirit; in the Mantegna print Jupiter is shown threatening to impale rebellious mankind on it.

Cornelius Agrippa says that the number twelve is of grace and perfection, a divine number.

The Hanged Man symbolizes change to a new and higher point of view, expansion of consciousness.

13. Death
Saturn in Capricorn

Visconti-Sforza

Marseille

Death is shown as a skeleton, the bare bones from which life has withdrawn, with the severing of the soul from the body and the ending of a phase in the cycle of life and death. Often he is reaping with the scythe of Time: popes, kings, queens, all fall to him. He clears the ground for new life.

In the Visconti-Sforza pack *Death* is shown as an archer. Here is the beginning of the red ground of the sphere of Fire, to pass through, which will lead to the life beyond death, the world of immortality, the Realm of Eternity.

This is the province of Saturn as ruler of Capricorn, cardinal and earthy. The association of death with Saturn, the oldest of the planetary gods, was traditional; he puts a limit to life. Sometimes Saturn was called a black sun; Capricorn is the southern limit of the sun's annual travel and in the northern hemisphere this is the death of the solar year. In classical myth Capricorn was called the Gate of the Gods, the gate through which the soul had to pass on its return to the heavens

after incarnation on Earth.

The Chariot and *Death* form a pair of polar opposites, life and death. *The Chariot* was the solar card showing the life spirit entering the body and animating it, vivifying it, giving it the power of movement. *Death* shows the withdrawing of the life spirit, the hardening and rigidity which will bring the end of the physical cycle. They repeat at a higher level the contrast in the first set between the young man, *The Magician,* and the old man, *The Hermit.*

Death can also be regarded as forming a contrasting pair with its neighbour, *The Hanged Man;* here is the outcome and conclusion of the sacrifice shown there.

The number thirteen, following the perfection of twelve, has always been associated with death. It was a reminder of the Last Supper of Christ with his twelve apostles.

Death is the ending of one cycle and the preparation for a new life.

14. Temperance
(Chronico)
The angel of the moon

Visconti-Sforza   Marseille

Temperance is shown as a woman pouring from one vessel down into another. She may wear the halo or the crown of a Virtue. Often she has angel's wings.

The two meanings of *Temperance* in the tarot have been discussed in Chapter 7. In one sense, from the standpoint of the microcosm, man, as one of the four Cardinal Virtues her power was essentially a moral one, being concerned with self-restraint, moderation, sobriety, chastity and so on (originally the lady had been mixing water with her wine). It was in such a sense that she had been given a part in the procession of the Triumph of Chastity.

But there was another sense, now from the macrocosmic point of view, in which *Temperance* was concerned with the tempering of the elements which were the basis of all creation and thus with the organizing and ordering of the generative powers of the cosmos, to bring about the ever-repeated cycle of life and death. It was this other sense that she was given when she was moved up in the new standard order of the trumps to position number 14, immediately above *Death*. One of the new cards in the Visconti-Sforza pack, she is shown there with

her dress patterned with the stars of heaven. She stands above the red cliffs; she is an immortal. She is now one of the forms of the Triple Goddess of the moon, the goddess who by her incarnation on Earth as Ceres or Diana or the Great Mother bridges the crucial gap between the translunar world of Eternity and the sublunar worlds of Time.

She is not the spirit of life, which is represented by *The Chariot*. Nor is she the spirit of *Death*, the withdrawal of the life-force from the body. She is, rather, the power that orders and controls both these in the perpetual cycle of regeneration, for ever creating new life to replace dead forms.

At the end of the first set of the trumps, the Realm of Man, and forming the link to the second set, there was *Love*, the winged angel Cupid, the angel of generation who brought down from Heaven the procreative and generative power of the cosmos and gave it physical expression at the individual level, through man and woman. At the end of this second set, the Realm of the Soul, and forming the link to the third set, the same theme is found in *Temperance*, the winged angel who again brings down the generative power of the cosmos but now at the level of Nature, the Great Mother, love at the level of humankind rather than of the individual. This is where Time has been brought into the allegory of the scheme of things which is the tarot. As the goddess Natura, the Earth Mother, *Temperance* controls the earthly side of the lunar frontier between Eternity and Time. She governs the power of solution and dissolution, life and death; she pours the life spirit from eternity, timelessness, down into an unending series of forms within the spheres of Time.

Temperance is closely akin to the Chronico of the Mantegna prints, where the winged angel holds the dragon of Time devouring its own tail, again a symbol of the perpetual regenerative cycle of Nature.

The giving to spirit of bodily substance was one of the powers of the moon. In the first set this had been exercised by *The Magician,* a lunar figure who had the power of materializing things at the physical level. Here in the second set the power is controlled at the generic level by *Temperance,* the angel of the moon.

Cornelius Agrippa says that fourteen, 'doth typifie Christ, who the fourteenth day of the first month was sacrificed for us'. The underlying meaning is of the ending of one era and the beginning of a new one.

Temperance is a card of regeneration, the power of the spirit to bring eternal renewal of life, through love.

Third Set
Trumps 15 to 21 (see Table 6)

The Triumphs of Petrarch out of which the tarot had originally arisen could be looked on almost as a kind of morality play, ending with the poet's vision of being reunited with Laura in heaven at the end of time. But the new tarot sequence which eventually became accepted as the standard order aimed at presenting not merely a morality but a whole world picture, a whole cosmology.

The first two sets of the trumps now represented the Realm of Man and the Realm of the Soul, both concerned with life in the sublunar worlds while the soul was still in the body and subject to the bonds of Time. The third set shows the Realm of Eternity, the life after *Death*, the life after the soul has withdrawn from the body and has been freed from Time.

The tarot grew up in the ambience of Renaissance humanism with its great revival of interest in classical antiquity, which had come to be looked on as something of a golden age. The classical myths were now given long moralized interpretations to harmonize them with Christian teachings. In the third set of trumps in particular there is much of this rather strange synthesis of Christian theology and pagan mythology which was so strong a feature of the period. Many of the cards here seem deliberately intended to bear both Christian and moralized pagan interpretations.

As a Christian version, there is *The Devil* waiting to pounce on the souls of sinners and roast them in Hell. *The Tower* shows both the Fall of Man and a hell-mouth, the way to and from Hell. *The Star* offers the promise of redemption, whether as the star in the east heralding the birth of Christ or as the Virgin. *The Moon* brings the birth to pass. The three final cards show the Trinity: *The Sun* as the Holy Spirit in Christ, *Judgement* as Christ the King in triumph, *The World* as the cosmos of God the Father; these present too the apocalyptic drama of the Last Things, the soul

rising up to the Sun of justice, and the resurrection of the dead at the Last Judgement, when the righteous shall have eternal glory in the new world to come.

As a pagan myth, Pluto, *The Devil*, abducts Proserpine, *The Star*. Her mother Ceres, *Temperance*, in her grief abandons her duty as the Great Mother, and Earth becomes a barren and a desolate place. On the edict of Jupiter, the King of Heaven *(Judgement)*, Pluto is forced to agree to release Proserpine, but only if she has not tasted food while in Hell. But Ascalaphus has seen her eating some pomegranate seeds — seeds which carry all the potential fertility of the Underworld. Because of this Proserpine can no longer be treated as Kore the girl, the virgin, she is now the Queen of Hell, wife of Pluto; and so she can be permitted to return to the upper world for only part of the year. Mercury, the messenger of Jupiter, is sent each year to conduct her back through the hell-mouth, *The Tower*.

When Proserpine comes back from the Underworld she brings with her the moisture which will restore fertility; as *The Star*, Venus, she brings together *The Moon*, the Lady of Generation, and *The Sun*, the Lord of Generation. The rule of law *(Judgement)* has been restored. Ceres is placated and the cycle of life starts up again. *The World* is made new once more.

The myth of the Triple Goddess, Luna *(The Moon)*, Proserpine *(The Star)* and Ceres the Great Mother *(Temperance)* thus offers an elegant expansion of the Proserpine theme. By her triple form she bridges the chasms between the worlds and links them through the processes of generation; as Trivia she commands the three ways, to Heaven, to Hell, and to Earth.

Renaissance humanism brought renewed interest in Neoplatonism, and the works of Plutarch (first to second century AD) once again became well known. In his dialogue *On*

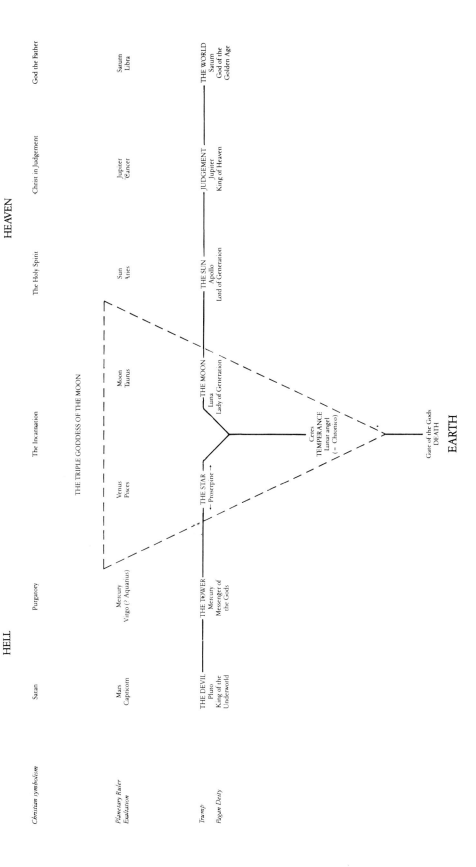

Realm of Eternity

HEAVEN

HELL

Christian symbolism	Satan	Purgatory	The Incarnation	The Holy Spirit	Christ in Judgement	God the Father

THE TRIPLE GODDESS OF THE MOON

Planetary Ruler Exaltation	Mars Capricorn	Mercury Virgo (? Aquarius)	Venus Pisces	Moon Taurus	Sun Aries	Jupiter Cancer	Saturn Libra

Trump Pagan Deity	THE DEVIL Pluto King of the Underworld	THE TOWER Mercury Messenger of the Gods	THE STAR ← Proserpine →	THE MOON Luna Lady of Generation	THE SUN Apollo Lord of Generation	JUDGEMENT Jupiter King of Heaven	THE WORLD Saturn God of the Golden Age

Ceres
TEMPERANCE
Lunar angel
(= Chronico)

Gate of the Gods
DEATH
EARTH

Table 6. The Astrology of the Trumps — Third Set.

the Face in the Moon (Moralia, 943-5) he relates an ancient tale connected with the myths of Proserpine and Pluto, that man undergoes two deaths. The first of these, brought about by Ceres, is when the soul leaves the body. The soul then wanders for a time in the regions between the Earth and the moon. The more sinful souls have to serve their punishment there, in Hades, hell or purgatory, while the more virtuous rest a while in limbo, Pluto's meadows. The second death comes when the soul at last rises up further to the moon, and Proserpine then brings about a dissolution in which the mind separates out from the soul:

> It is separated by love for the image in the sun through which shines forth manifest the desirable and fair and divine and blessed towards which all nature in one way or another yearns, for it must be out of love for the sun that the moon herself goes her round and gets into conjunction with him in her yearning to receive from him what is most fructifying. (Loeb translation.)

The more material elements of the soul remain on the moon. The process of generation is eventually continued by the sun with his vital force sowing mind again in the moon, who produces new souls for which Earth furnishes bodies. The moon thus both takes and gives, joins together and divides. She is the necessary middle term in the process of generation.

Something rather like this story seems to have been in the mind of the designer of the standard order of the tarot, in his use of the Proserpine myth and the Triple Goddess of the moon. In the Visconti-Sforza pack *The Sun* (Figure 4) looks a strikingly apt

illustration of the 'love for the image in the sun' mentioned by Plutarch. A cherub, a cupid, rises on a cloud above the landscape of the moon, with the tower (the way up from Hell) in the background; he holds above him a radiant mask of the sun. At all events the story brings out very clearly the importance in Neoplatonist symbolism of the sun and the moon as the Lord and the Lady of Generation.

Astrologically the third set of the trumps corresponds to the planets in their signs of exaltation.

In the first two sets, representing the sublunar worlds ruled by time, the order of the cards had followed the sequence imposed by the order of the signs in the two zodiacal semicircles. In the third set, representing the Realm of Eternity, freed from time the order no longer follows the zodiacal sequence. *The Moon* (moon in Taurus) holds the central position, ruling the three ways which lead to Heaven, to Hell, and to Earth. *The Star*, Proserpine, immediately below her, brings the moisture of Venus in Pisces to *The Moon* and *The Sun*.

The four cardinal signs of the zodiac were regarded as initiating the influences of the four elements to which they correspond. The three highest trumps — those which represent the Christian Trinity, *The Sun, Judgement, The World* — correspond to the planets exalted in the first three cardinal signs: sun in Aries, Jupiter in Cancer, Saturn in Libra respectively. The fourth cardinal sign, Capricorn the Goat-fish, falls to *The Devil*, Satan. Mercury as the messenger of the gods rules *The Tower*, the hell-mouth communicating between Hell and the upper world.

15. The Devil
Mars in Capricorn

Hebreo (16c.)

Marseille

The Devil is both the Christian Satan and the pagan Pluto, King of the Underworld, Hades.

Later cards such as the Marseille design may show him as androgynous. In early cards he is quite definitely male; often he has an extra face in his tummy, to show that like all proper devils his mind is firmly centred on lower things. Minchiate designs show him with hissing serpents around his loins.

Usually he has bat-like wings; he had been an angel. He may have the horns and ears and lower parts of a goat, or the feet and claws of a harpy. He may have a pitchfork, to help with the roasting of souls in Hell, or a burning torch.

In the Christian story he was a fallen angel. He had been thrown out of Heaven, and he appears in the tarot as the lowest card of the third set, in the place to which he fell, bottom of the class, in Hell. His sins had been pride and disobedience, and it was these into which he tried to tempt mankind, disrupting the proper order of things in the divinely ordered hierarchy.

In the classical myth Pluto with the connivance of his brother Jupiter had seized

Proserpine (= *The Star*) while she was gathering flowers in a meadow and had carried her off down to the Underworld as his wife. After a certain amount of fuss she began to settle down with Pluto, but her mother Ceres (= *Temperance*) went around the Earth wailing and desperately searching for her daughter. In her despair Ceres abandoned her duties as the Great Mother, and the Earth became a sterile and desolate place. The proper order of things had broken down.

In the Visconti-Sforza pack *The Devil* is missing, but if he were another of the new cards by the later artist he might have been shown as Pluto so as to complete the theme of the Rape of Proserpine; in which form he was in fact presented in a sixteenth-century 'classical' pack (Dummett, plate 17).

Whether taken in the Christian or the pagan sense there seems no difficulty in attributing *The Devil* to Mars in his sign of exaltation, Capricorn, cardinal and earthy, the sign of the goat-fish.

The Devil is a card of energy and ambition and pride; it is the very strength of these which cause disruption and trouble.

16. The Tower
Mercury in Virgo

Charles VI   Marseille

The Tower is both the Tower of Babel of Christian legend and also a pagan hell-mouth.

The building of the Tower of Babel was a mark of the presumptuousness shown by mankind in later ages, after Adam and Eve had once been tempted by Satan (himself a fallen angel) into those first acts of pride and disobedience which were the Fall of Man. God brought about the destruction of the Tower by causing its builders to suffer confusion of tongues, depicted in the Marseille pattern by tongues of flame or lightning from Heaven striking its crown, its head; figures of the builders are shown falling from it. Sometimes the card shows Adam in the Garden of Eden with the beasts of the field, under the Tree of Knowledge of Good and Evil (*Genesis,* 2) with the lightning striking it (Kaplan, p.152., Dummett, plates 27, 30, 31). The Minchiate pattern shows the expulsion of Adam and Eve from the Garden (Kaplan, pp.51, 52). But in all these the theme is in essence the same, the punishment of sin by God.

The card is missing from the Visconti-Sforza pack, but other early versions often show a dark entrance or doorway in the tower.

Then the emphasis is on it as a hell-mouth, in pagan legend one of the entrances through which souls had to pass on their way down to the Underworld.

Mercury was the psychopomp, the guide of souls, whose task it was to guide souls between the worlds in accordance with the orders of Heaven. When Jupiter eventually gave in to the imploring and incessant demands of Ceres for the return of her daughter, it was his son and messenger Mercury who was sent down to the Underworld to fetch Proserpine back from Pluto.

Mercury was thus in effect the guardian of the threshold and could be regarded as the keeper of *The Tower,* the entrance through which they had to pass. He was usually said to have his exaltation in Virgo, mutable and earthy, though it is occasionally given as Aquarius. In the second set Mercury had been charged with the administration of *Justice,* through its realization in the human soul. Here in the third set as the planetary lord of *The Tower,* Mercury is concerned with the administration of divine justice, symbolized by the thunder and lightning, acts of God.

The Tower is a card of punishment and

confusion, the divine justice which is to strike those who have succumbed to the wiles of Satan. It was sometimes called the House of the Devil. But the damnation is not necessarily eternal; *The Star,* Proserpine, shows there is a way of salvation.

17. The Star
Venus in Pisces

Visconti-Sforza

Marseille

The Star is both the Christian Star of Bethlehem and also Proserpine herself.

Originally the card had represented the Fame, of Petrarch's Triumph of Fame. Petrarch himself had compared Fame to the morning star, Venus, coming from the east before the rising sun. Early cards show it as the star in the east heralding the birth of Christ, seen by the three wise men or magi or kings. Sometimes there are one or more of the three kings, sometimes astrologers gazing up at the star and making calculations, sometimes just a star. In the later packs which follow the standard order, *The Star* usually shows Proserpine herself.

Worn down by the pleading of Ceres, Jupiter eventually came to an arrangement with his brother Pluto, King of the Underworld, that Proserpine should be allowed to return to the upper world provided she had not tasted any food while in Hell. But it came to light that she had picked a pomegranate there and had eaten some of its seeds. By this she had taken into herself something of the fertile nature of the Underworld and so had become irrevocably wedded to Pluto; she could not be allowed to

leave him for ever. At last a compromise was reached between the parties that she would spend a third of each year with Pluto and for the remaining months she could come back to stay with her mother Ceres. With her return she brings the rain and the moisture which makes the Earth fertile again. Ceres again takes up her duties as the Great Mother, and the wheel of life and death turns once more.

In the Visconti-Sforza pack Proserpine, *The Star,* (Figure 3) is shown in a dress patterned with stylized rain clouds and wearing a reversible cape of red and green, the red to signify the parched earth during the hot summer months when she is away in the Underworld, the green the fertility which will come back with her return. But her feet are stockinged. Because of the pomegranate seeds she may not freely tread the ground of Heaven; as one of the three forms of the Triple Goddess she still looks towards her left, the left hand path which leads down to Hades, Hell. (In her other two forms the Goddess is shown as *The Moon* looking up to her right, towards Heaven, and as *Temperance* (Ceres) down to Earth.)

Cards of the Marseille pattern show

Proserpine bringing back the moisture and fertility to Earth. Her eating of the pomegranate seeds had been seen by Ascalaphus, and it was he who told about it. Ceres, in her fury with him for this changed him into an owl, and so a bird is often shown in the card.

The Sun and *The Moon* are the Lord and the Lady of Generation. But something is needed to bring them together; this is the moisture of Venus, the moisture which Proserpine brings on her return. *The Star* is Proserpine both as the Venus, immaculate, who brings *The Sun* and *The Moon* together in Heaven, and also as the Venus who goes back each year to Hell, where as the wife of Pluto, *The Devil,* she is the Queen of the Underworld, the dark Venus.

In Christian allegory the star in the east was often identified with Venus as the morning star which rose before the sun, Christ; and as the Virgin, *The Star,* carries the promise of the Redemption which will deliver mankind from the Fall shown in the previous card, *The Tower.* Perhaps too there is also something of the idea that after death the soul needs first to go for a while for purification before ascending further to Heaven; this is purgatory, or Pluto's meadows.

Astrologically the attribution of the card to Venus thus fits well, both from the Christian aspect and mythologically with Proserpine-Venus mated with Pluto-Mars. The power of Venus is strengthened in her sign of exaltation, Pisces, a mutable and watery sign.

The Star is a card of promise of new life, fertility, and of redemption and salvation. But it can also be a card of regression into a more primitive, instinctual life.

The Star as Proserpine, Queen of the Underworld, with Ascalaphus. (Fifteenth-century hand painted card, Victoria and Albert Museum, London).

18. The Moon
Moon in Taurus

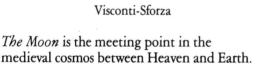

Visconti-Sforza   Marseille

The Moon is the meeting point in the medieval cosmos between Heaven and Earth.

Originally the card had been part of Petrarch's Triumph of Time. The sun and the moon were the time-keepers of antiquity. They were not Time itself, which belonged to Saturn, but they controlled him, they drove him on.

The sun, Apollo, controlled the movements of all the other planets and so governed all the cycles of time of longer duration, the seasons, the year, a lifetime, cosmic time.

The moon, the twin sister and the servant of the sun, carried out his more immediate wishes, giving effect to them from month to month, from day to day, from hour to hour. She governed the shorter cycles of time. In Minchiate cards this is symbolized by a clockface.

Since the moon was nearer the Earth and her apparent motion much faster than the sun's, her influence on day-to-day matters was regarded as much greater. She was the main short-term factor to be considered in health and sickness, in growth and decline, as well as in the more mutable terrestrial conditions like the tides and the weather. The day-to-day

course of events on Earth was to be prognosticated by the position of the moon in the zodiac and the aspects she would make to the other planets; and early trumps based on the Petrarchan poem, such as the Charles VI card, show astrologers measuring the position of the moon for this purpose. They measure Time.

As the lowest of the planets and the one nearest Earth, the sphere of the moon formed the crucial boundary between Heaven and Earth, the frontier between Eternity and the worlds of Time and form, between the celestial world of Aether and the spheres composed of the other four elements, Fire, Air, Water and Earth. An early woodcut card shows *The Moon* riding in the sky above stylized representations of the spheres of Fire and Air, the two elements forming the middle world, the world of the soul.

After *Death,* the soul ascends through *Temperance,* the goddess of life and death. It may then take either the left-hand path to Hell, or the right-hand path to Heaven, according to its state of grace.

In the Visconti-Sforza pack, regarded as a Christian sequence, *The Star* had brought the

The Moon. Rosenwald Collection, National Gallery of Art, Washington, D.C.

promise of redemption from the Fall of Man, through the Incarnation. *The Moon* shows Mary, the Mother of God, the vessel through whom the Incarnation of Christ is given bodily form.

In pagan terms, the Triple Goddess (Figure 3) is the ruler of the crossroads. As *Temperance,* Ceres the Great Mother, she commands the way down to Earth. As *The Star,* Proserpine, she governs the way to Hell. As *The Moon* she rules the way up to Heaven.

The Moon here wears a violet-purple mantle bearing the triple golden rays of the solar trinity; she looks to her right, to the right-hand path which leads up to her twin brother and lord, *The Sun. The Tower,* the entrance to Hell, lies behind her, on her left. With her bare feet she touches the ground of Heaven; she is herself of aethereal nature. She is the Lady of Generation, primal matter.

In the Marseille pattern *The Moon* is shown presiding over the crossroads and giving rays of Fire and Air, the elements of the middle world through which the soul may ascend to Heaven. But beneath the moon lies the terraqueous world, the world of the lower elements Earth and Water and of the instinctual life symbolized by the hounds of Diana and the crayfish of Cancer; the soul who has become involved here will be driven to take the path between the two frontier towers leading down to Hell, the Underworld of Pluto.

In the planetary framework the card can be given its natural attribution, the moon. The sign of its exaltation, Taurus, fixed and earthy, would signify the primal earth, the primal matter needed for fertility and generation.

The Moon stands at the crossroads between Heaven and Hell and Earth; she offers the soul the choice of ways.

19. The Sun
Sun in Aries

Visconti-Sforza   Marseille

The Sun appears in the tarot in many and varied forms but the underlying theme is always the sun as a symbol of the life-force; it is a visible sign of God and of his love.

Like *The Moon, The Sun* had originally arisen out of Petrarch's Triumph of Time; they were the two timekeepers of the universe. The Charles VI card shows the sun shining down on one of the three Fates, Clotho, who spins the thread of life and who presides especially over the moment of Time of birth, which astrologically determines the destiny of a life. Here is the beginning of the creation of the human soul, and with it the beginnings of death. 'In our birth lies our death, our end depends on our beginning' (inscription in Figure 6, from Manilius). Cards of the Bologna style still show the figure of Clotho spinning her thread (Kaplan. pp.115, 128, 50., Dummett, plates 18, 20).

A design preserved in Minchiate packs shows the sun shining down on two lovers no longer young, perhaps Petrarch reunited with Laura at the end of Time (Kaplan, p.52).

Another type of the card shows *The Sun* as Apollo the sun god, with the lyre on which he plays the music of the spheres; he controls the movements of the planets, and Time (Kaplan, p.54).

The Este card shows Diogenes in his tub, telling Alexander the Great to move out of the way so as not to block the sunlight; even the greatest of worldly powers cannot stop the cosmic life-force (Kaplan, pp.117-8., Dummett, plate 9).

Yet a further version shows a girl looking at herself in a mirror held up by an ape, symbolizing the vanity of worldly things; the light of the sun shows things as they really are and gives true vision of God's universe (Kaplan, p.135).

The Belgian pattern rings the changes by allotting Clotho to *The Moon*. The archangel Michael, as *The Sun*, waves his banner with the red cross and chases off to fight the dragon, Satan; he was the protector of Christians against the devil, and in the hour of death leads their souls to God (Kaplan, p.284).

The Visconti-Sforza form of *The Sun* (Figure 4) shows a cherub on a cloud riding above the lunar landscape and holding aloft a rayed mask representing Christ as the visible face of God. It must remind us also of the legend from Plutarch, that the more spiritual elements of the soul were to be separated out from the more material ones 'by love for the image in the sun'.

The Visconti-Sforza pack here brings in a further instance of Group Coding: the three final cards, *The Sun, Judgement* and *The World,* all show angels, cherubs or putti; here we are in the empyrean, the sphere of Heaven. The three cards represent the Christian Trinity, with *The Sun* as the Holy Spirit or Christ the Logos, *Judgement* as Christ the King, and *The World* as the new world to come, the City of God, symbol of God the Father. Here too is the apocalyptic drama of the Last Days, with the last three cards showing the divine omnipotence which must finally overcome the forces of sin, *The Devil* and *The Tower.*

Around the end of the fifteenth century there appeared the version of *The Sun* adopted later in the Marseille pattern, showing two children playing together. I think the meaning is to be found in *Matthew* 18.3: 'Except ye turn, and become as little children, ye shall in no wise enter into the kingdom of heaven'. In the new standard sequence the soul rising after *Death* would come to the crossroads of *The Moon.* From there the left-hand path leads down to Hell. Turning onto the right-hand path, *The Sun* is the entrance to the kingdom of Heaven.

Looking at the symbolism from the pagan angle, in the Mantegna series the sun had been shown among the planets, as print A44, and his special task as Lord of Generation had been delegated to his angel Cosmico (print B 33). In the tarot trumps, with only twenty-one cards against the fifty prints of the Mantegna series, there was not room for both figures separately. The duty of Cosmico as Lord of Generation is here performed by *The Sun* itself.

The Sun shows strongly the strange mixing of Christian and pagan symbolism which was a mark of the humanism of Renaissance Italy. But so far as our planetary framework is concerned the allocation of the card is straightforward, to its natural correspondence the sun. The cardinal sign Aries, the exaltation of the sun and the first sign of the zodiac, would show that here is the beginning of the creative and generative cycle which leads to birth on Earth. Here too is where the soul enters back into Heaven, from whence it came.

The Sun is a card of the life-force and of love as the power behind all creation, 'the love which moves the sun and the other stars' (Dante).

20. Judgement
Jupiter in Cancer

Visconti-Sforza   Marseille

Judgement is shown in the tarot in purely Christian terms, with one or more angels sounding their trumpets to awaken the dead and summon them to the Last Judgement.

In the Steele list the card is called *The Angel*. This name is also generally used with packs stemming from the Charles VI type of order, such as the Bologna pattern.

The card had originally arisen out of Petrarch's Triumph of Eternity, the final one of the cycle of poems. In this the poet has first a vision of the new world, changeless and eternal and in which Time itself (the previous Triumph) shall be overcome and have no more power. It is only after this vision that he goes on to muse on the eventual coming of the Last Judgement, after which his love for Laura shall be rewarded by seeing her again in Heaven.

The Charles VI order follows exactly this sequence, with *The World* coming first and Judgement *(The Angel)* as the final card.

In the Visconti-Sforza pack, *Judgement* (Figure 4) shows the two angels with their trumpets heralding Christ the King, who bears a crown, orb and sword and is to preside at the Last Judgement. From the red ground of the tomb the dead rise up to immortality.

It is one of the original 'Bembo' cards and it may have been the red ground here which gave the designer of the new cards the idea of using red earth as a mark of discontinuity to indicate the separation of worlds and to show immortality.

Probably the Visconti-Sforza pack had originally followed the Charles VI type of order in which *The Angel* is the final card, but in the reorganized sequence the last two cards were transposed so that *Judgement (The Angel)* came first and *The World* now became the final card, the order which eventually became the standard one.

This transposition would have had two advantages. It would allow *Judgement* to be matched up tidily with Christ the King as the second person of the Trinity, and *The World*, the City of God, with God the Father as the senior person of the Trinity. It would also have fitted much better into an astrological scheme, since it would present a neat sequence of *The Sun* exalted in Aries, the first of the cardinal signs (which are traditionally of initiating nature), *Judgement* as Jupiter exalted in Cancer, the second of the cardinal signs, and *The World* as Saturn exalted in

Libra, the third of the cardinal signs.

For our framework the allocation of *Judgement,* Christ the King, to Jupiter, King of Heaven, seems right. The sign Cancer, the exaltation of Jupiter, would stress the quality of mercy in the Judge.

Judgement is a card of renewal, rebirth, awakening to higher consciousness. It is also a card of the forgiveness of sins — at least, if they are only fairly little ones. Grossly unrepentant sinners are sent down to *The Tower.*

21. The World
Saturn in Libra

Visconti-Sforza   Marseille

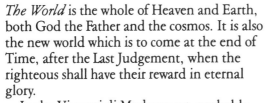

The World is the whole of Heaven and Earth, both God the Father and the cosmos. It is also the new world which is to come at the end of Time, after the Last Judgement, when the righteous shall have their reward in eternal glory.

In the Visconti di Modrone set, probably the earliest of the three 'Bembo' packs, the card depicts a woman in Heaven, above a scene on Earth. She holds a crown and a trumpet, to show that she has gained immortal fame. Perhaps she is Petrarch's Laura. (Kaplan, p.92.)

Other early forms of the card stemming from the Triumph of Eternity show an angel above a landscape. (Kaplan, pp.117-8, 130., Dummett, plates 5, 6, 9.) In the Charles VI cards the figure seems to represent Prudence, often regarded as the highest of the Cardinal Virtues (see Figure 2). Sometimes the figure depicted is Mercury, the messenger of the gods, controlling the four elements. (Kaplan, p.128., Dummett, plate 18.) Sometimes the figure is the goddess Fortuna with her sail. (Kaplan, pp.135, 152, 284., Dummett, plates 27, 30.)

The Visconti-Sforza card is one of the new

ones by the later hand. It shows a walled city on an island, brought down from Heaven by two cherubs wearing scarves bearing the triple golden rays of the sun. This is the New Jerusalem, Christ's kingdom to be established on Earth. It is also the City of God. The island brings in the motif of the red cliffs of immortality. The stars shine brightly in the sky, to signify that here the four elements of Fire, Air, Water and Earth are under the control of the divine fifth element, Aether.

In this card the small embossed gold panels of the background are here squared up, suggesting that the four elements are now made stable by the fifth element, the circle of aether. In every other trump of the Visconti-Sforza pack the background panels are arranged diagonally. The distinction looks to have been introduced deliberately, to signify that the card was the final one completing both the third set and the series, in a sense standing outside the others. The Steele sermon had told us that *The World* could also be taken as God the Father. The Visconti-Sforza card too symbolizes both God the Father as the Creator, and Paradise.

This final card in the series of the trumps

must always have presented a very special problem for the designer, symbolizing as it had to do both the First Cause and also the supreme end of man's spiritual quest.

Victoria & Albert
Museum, London

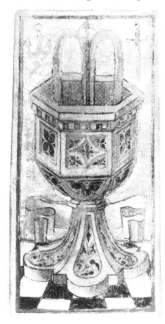

Guildhall, London

A rare type of hand-painted card shows the Grail, the mystical chalice which had received the blood of Christ, with an arrow representing the lance which had pierced his side at the crucifixion eternally sending forth a fountain of blood, the life blood of the cosmos. Often confused with the Ace of Cups, the black-and-white checked floor in the Guildhall and Goldschmidt examples of the card shows that it is a trump, rather than an Ace. The Guildhall specimen has also a sword and an anchor, symbols of the Fisher King and standing for the other two hallows of the Grail legends, which were well known and popular in fifteenth-century Italy. Another version of this type, in the Victoria & Albert Museum, has two cherubs like those in *The World* of the Visconti-Sforza pack, symbols of Heaven and again showing that the card is a trump, not an Ace.

Symbolizing as it does the ultimate value, the Holiest of Holies, there is only one place in the trump series that could have been given

to the Grail: the highest position. It was a variant of *The World.*

The Marseille pattern shows a girl dancing, within an oval garland. At the four corners are the four living creatures of the Apocalypse, symbols also of the four elements, signifying that here we are at the Last Day, in the Realm of Eternity. Perhaps the girl is the spirit of Aether, the divine fifth element. Perhaps she is *anima mundi,* the Soul of the World. Perhaps she is Psyche, the human soul perfected. Perhaps she is the Virgin as the second Eve, through whom the first Eve was redeemed.

In all the designs the underlying theme is essentially the same, the world made new and perfect.

The first of the trumps had shown *The Magician* at his table, with the symbols of the four elements in front of him which he could arrange, re-arrange, and combine at his will, to produce all the manifestations and illusions of the world of mutability. In the final card, *The World,* the four elements are again shown but now, instead of being under the control of a merely human figure, they are under the rule of the fifth element, Aether, the spirit of the divine, to show the perfection of the cosmos at the end of Time.

In our framework *The World,* symbol of God the Father, can be allocated to Saturn, the Old God who had reigned before Jupiter. The exaltation of Saturn is the third of the cardinal signs, Libra, the scales of Justice, carrying with it perhaps a suggestion of the return of Astraea, goddess of Justice, and with her the return of the Golden Age.

The World is a card of great good fortune — in the end, when the ficklenesses of mundane fortune have been surmounted.

Here is the squaring of the circle; here the world of the quadrate four elements, the world of Time and mutability, is created from the circle, the perfect form, symbol of the divine.

Here too is the return movement, the making circular again of the square, the return of the four elements into the circle, in the realm of Eternity.

Here is eternal recurrence, moved by love.

The Fool

Visconti-Sforza

Marseille

The Fool is the simpleton, the halfwit, but he is also the clown, the jester, the wise man who achieves his end by wearing the garb of folly.

He is also zany, a bit of a rogue, a bit of a trickster, but there is wisdom in him.

He can be pure mindlessness, open to every influence, spiritual or sensual or worldly or simply foolish — perfect innocence yet total involvement.

He is the unpredictable, not to be confined within any framework. He is God's Providence.

He can assume any character, play every part.

He is Everyman, with all his possibilities.

Acknowledgements and Bibliography

A book of this kind must draw greatly on the works of others. This short bibliography may serve both to acknowledge the greatest of my debts and also to provide a basic list for further reading.

Two books have been particularly helpful for general reference:

Kaplan, Stuart R. *The Encyclopedia of Tarot* Vol. 1 (U.S. Games Systems, Inc., New York, 1978).
Especially valuable for its many illustrations of early tarot cards and for its documentary references. Includes an extensive bibliography.

Dummett, Michael *The Game of Tarot* (Duckworth, London, 1980).
Includes a very useful survey of early tarot packs and an important study of the various types of order of the trumps.

The main works which have been consulted for particular subjects are:

Chapter 1 The Playing-card Background

Campori, Giuseppe 'Le carte da giuoco dipinte per gli Estense nel seculo XV.' in *Atti e memorie,* serie i, vol.7, 1874, Dep. di Storia Patria, Modena.
Mentions the entry in the Este books for 1442, for the painting of trionfi cards.

Klein, Robert 'Les tarots enluminés du XVe siècle' in *L'Oeil,* issue for January, 1967, Paris. A valuable short study by a distinguished art historian.

Chapter 2 Ways of Approach

Hind, Arthur M. *Early Italian Engraving* 7 vols. (Bernard Quaritch Ltd., London, 1938-48).
Excellent reproductions of the Triumphs of Petrarch, the Tarocchi of Mantegna, and the Children of the Planets, with much background information.

Chapter 3. The Charles VI Pack

Menestrier, Claude F. *Bibliothèque curieuse et instructive,* 2 vols. (Estienne Ganeau, Trévoux, 1704).
Extracts from the royal household accounts for 1392 mentioning the payment to Gringonneur, painter, for three packs of cards.

Schreiber, Wilhelm Ludwig *Die ältesten Spielkarten* (J. H. E. Heitz, Strassburg, 1937).
Discusses the dating of the earliest tarot packs.

Chapter 4. The Visconti-Sforza Pack

Rasmo, Niccolò, 'Il Codice palatino 556 e le sue illustrazioni.' in *Rivista d'Arte,* Anno XXI (Serie ii, Anno Xi), 1939, Florence.
Includes some reproductions of drawings in that manuscript.

Gardner, Edmund G. *The Arthurian Legend in Italian Literature* (J. M. Dent Ltd., London, 1930).
Shows that the Grail legends were widely known in medieval Italy. Includes some further reproductions from Cod. pal. 556.

Chapter 5. The Original Story

Moakley, Gertrude 'The Tarot Trumps and Petrarch's Trionfi.' in *Bulletin of The New York Public Library,* vol.60, No.2, February 1956.

Moakley, Gertrude *The Tarot Cards painted by Bonifacio Bembo* (The New York Public Library, New York, 1966).
Both the above are essential reading.

Levenson, J. A., Oberhuber, K., Sheehan, J. L. *Early Italian Engravings from the National Gallery of Art* (National Gallery of Art, Washington, 1973).
Mentions the great importance of Petrarch's Trionfi in art.

Wilkins, Ernest H. (trans.) *The Triumphs of Petrarch* (University of Chicago Press, Chicago, 1962).
An excellent modern translation.

Carnicelli, D. D. (ed.) *Lord Morley's Tryumphes of Fraunces Petrarcke* (Harvard University Press, Cambridge, Mass., 1971).
A sixteenth-century translation with a useful introduction, bibliography and illustrations.

Chapter 6. The Three Worlds

Heninger, S. K. *The Cosmographical Glass* (The Huntington Library, San Marino, California, 1977).
Renaissance diagrams of the universe.

Yates, Frances A. *The Art of Memory* (Routledge and Kegan Paul, London, 1966).
Includes valuable material on the Virtues, especially Prudence.

Chapter 7. The Angels of Generation

Thorndike, Lynn *The Sphere of Sacrobosco and its Commentators* (University of Chicago Press, Chicago, 1949).
Includes text and translation of *De Sphaera.*

Bottari, Stefano 'I Tarocchi di Castello Ursino' in *Emporium,* vol.114, 1951, Bergamo.
The Catania tarot cards.

Economou, George D. *The Goddess Natura in Medieval Literature* (Harvard University Press, Cambridge, Mass., 1972).

Nitzsche, Jane C. *The Genius Figure in Antiquity and the Middle Ages* (Columbia University Press, New York, 1975).
The last two books contain much material on figures of generation, though not specifically mentioning the Tarocchi of Mantegna.

Chapter 8. The Children of the Planets

Lippmann, Friedrich *The Seven Planets* International Chalcographical Society, London, 1895 (also a German edition, Berlin, 1895).
Reproductions of six sets of the Children of the Planets.

Kenton, Warren *Astrology. The Celestial Mirror* (Thames and Hudson, London, 1974).
An excellent short study of astrology written from the historical standpoint. Many illustrations, including the Children of the Planets.

Chapter 9. The Planetary Gods

In the fifteenth century the most important single source of classical mythology was Ovid. However he was extensively moralized and commented on, and bits were taken from many other sources, particularly from the rather rambling manual of Boccaccio, which itself frequently gave several conflicting versions of the genealogy of the gods. Consequently it is often difficult or impossible to find any entirely agreed version. With this qualification, probably as good a version as any, of the stories as known in the Renaissance is:

King, William *Heathen Gods and Heroes* B. Lintott, London, 1710, reprinted Centaur Press Ltd., London 1965.

The standard work on the general uses of mythology in Renaissance art and literature is:

Seznec, Jean *The Survival of the Pagan Gods* (Pantheon Books Inc., New York, 1953).

Chapter 10. The Structure of the Tarot Trumps

Renaissance astrology was based on the seven planets then known. Modern textbooks of astrology, based on the ten planets including Uranus, Neptune and Pluto, are consequently of only rather limited value for our special purposes here. A useful book summarizing the technical assumptions of the older astrology is:

Eade, J. C. *The Forgotten Sky* (Clarendon Press, Oxford, 1984).

Amongst popular textbooks, one which gives greater weight than most to the standpoints of the older astrology is:

McCaffery, Ellen *Graphic Astrology* Macoy Publishing Company, New York and L. N. Fowler & Co. Ltd., London, 1952.

A very good textbook using a modern approach but also including some historical background material is:

Parker, Derek and Julia *The New Compleat Astrologer* (Mitchell Beazley, London, 1984).

Chapter 11. Conclusions — and some guesses

Warburg, Aby 'Italienische Kunst und internationaler Astrologie im Palazzo Schifanoia zu Ferrara.' in his *Gesammelte Schriften*, 2 vols., B. G. Teubner, Leipzig, 1932, reprinted in 1 vol. Kraus, Liechtenstein, 1969.
Identifies Pellegrino Prisciani as the inspirer of the astrological frescoes at Ferrara.

Rotondò, Antonio 'Pellegrino Prisciani.' in *Rinascimento,* Anno Xi, No.i. 1960, Florence. Summarizes most of what is known about him.

Gundersheimer, Werner L. *Ferrara* (Princeton University Press, Princeton, 1973). Particularly useful for background material.

For illustrations I am grateful to:
The British Library, London
The Trustees of the British Museum, London
Stuart R. Kaplan and U.S. Games Systems, Inc., New York
Victoria & Albert Museum, London
The Warburg Institute, University of London
The Worshipful Company of Makers of Playing Cards

Index